THE FIRST FLIGHT
AROUND·THE·WORLD

APRIL 6 - SEPTEMBER 28, 1924

By **Carroll V. Glines** and **Stan Cohen**

1 Lt. Jack Harding
2 Lt. Leslie Arnold
3 Lt. H.H Ogden
4 Lt. Lowell H. Smith
5 Lt. Leigh Wade
6 Lt. Eric Nelson

Lt. Lowell Smith Commander of World Flight

PICTORIAL HISTORIES PUBLISHING COMPANY, INC.

L.C. Control Number 00 132221

ISBN 1-57510-072-X

First Printing: June 2000

*The cover illustration was done by Keith Meininger. Keith graduated from the
University of Nebraska and attended the Chouinard Art Institute in Los
Angeles. He worked in the art field for several corporations including
ABC Television and in 1954 went to work for the Douglas Aircraft
Company in Santa Monica, California, in their corporate com-
munications department. He retired from the McDonnell-
Douglas Company in 1987 and now lives in
Lincoln, Nebraska.*

Back cover photo of the New Orleans *courtesy of Peter M. Bowers.*
Cover Graphics: Egeler Design
Layout by Stan Cohen
Typography by Jan Taylor
Missoula, Montana

PICTORIAL HISTORIES PUBLISHING COMPANY, INC.
713 South Third West, Missoula, Montana 59801
Phone (406) 549-8488 FAX (406) 728-9280
phpc@montana.com

Introduction

When the fixed–wing flying machine reached the point where it could span distances of more than a few miles, it was inevitable that some intrepid airmen would look at the globe and consider it possible to circumnavigate it by air. The world had been proven round ever since Ferdinand Magellan set out from Spain on Sept. 20, 1519, in five ships and sailed southwestward around South America, then northwest to the Philippines. He was killed there, but his flagship *Victoria* continued westward and completed the first circumnavigation of the globe.

Many others circled the world by ship and in 1913, John Henry Mears has the distinction of being the first circumnavigator to fly. He flew only 40 miles of the trip but it was enough to make it different from the others.

World War I canceled any thoughts of flying around the world, but the war did have one beneficial effect: aircraft, engines and facilities all improved rapidly. Thousands of pilots were trained and a desire to continue to fly an "aeroplane" was instilled in the minds of many trained pilots that would not long be denied. In 1920, the Aero Club of America and the Aerial League of America jointly appointed a three–man commission to tour the world and organize the First Aerial Derby Around the World. They traveled more than 40,000 miles and visited 32 countries. The commission was dissolved by mutual consent and the World's Board of Aeronautical Commissions, Inc. was established in its place to organize the derby. Rules were drawn up and reflected an optimism about the future of aviation that was based on the fact that a few aircraft had already flown great distances without refueling and now seemed reliable enough to make such an arduous trip. The aspirations of the two aviation organizations were never realized, however. The world did not yet seem ready for such an undertaking, and the derby never went beyond the planning stage.

However, the thought lingered in the minds of many fliers all over the world in the first five years after the end of World War I. Fliers of at least five nations announced their intention to try, although none received any assistance from their governments. But, there were a few in the United States who thought such a flight was possible and should be attempted by Army Air Service pilots on active duty. This book is about those who were first to succeed.

"Other men will fly around the earth, but never again will anybody fly around it for the first time."
ADMIRAL ROBINSON, SAN DIEGO, 1924

Acknowledgments

This book could not have been completed without the generous help of many individuals and archives. They include the following:

- George Kirkman and Charles Schwartz, Museum of Flying, Santa Monica, California
- Peter M. Bowers, Seattle, Washington
- Dave Menard, U.S. Air Force Museum, Dayton, Ohio
- Hugh Morgan, Beavercreek, Ohio
- Jim Ruotsala, Juneau, Alaska
- Dennis Wrynn, Cutehogue, New York
- Janice Baker and Katherine Williams, Museum of Flight, Seattle, Washington
- Al Lloyd, Bellevue, Washington
- Mel Brown, Austin, Texas
- Bob White, Fredericksburg, Virginia
- Linda Brisco, Harry Ransom Humanities Research Center, University of Texas at Austin
- Alex Spencer and the staff of National Air & Space Museum, Washington, D.C.
- Ted Spencer, Alaska Aviation Heritage Museum, Anchorage, Alaska
- Staff of Alaska State Library, Juneau, Alaska
- Larry Syplot, Morgantown, West Virginia
- Dusty Finley, Eagle River, Alaska
- Lowell Thomas Jr. and John Cloe, Anchorage, Alaska
- Jake Ellison, Burton, Ohio
- Frederick Cortez, History and Traditions Museum, Lackland AFB, San Antonio, Texas

Also of valuable assistance was Duane J. Reed, Chief, Special Collections Department, U.S. Air Force Academy, Colorado Springs, Colorado, and the staff of the National Archives, Washington, D.C. A special thanks goes to Major John Beaulieu, USAF, a graduate student at Auburn University. His doctoral dissertation on the world flight helped provide some of the personal information and led us to many of the photographs that would otherwise not have been obtained.

The Authors

PETER M. BOWERS

Contents

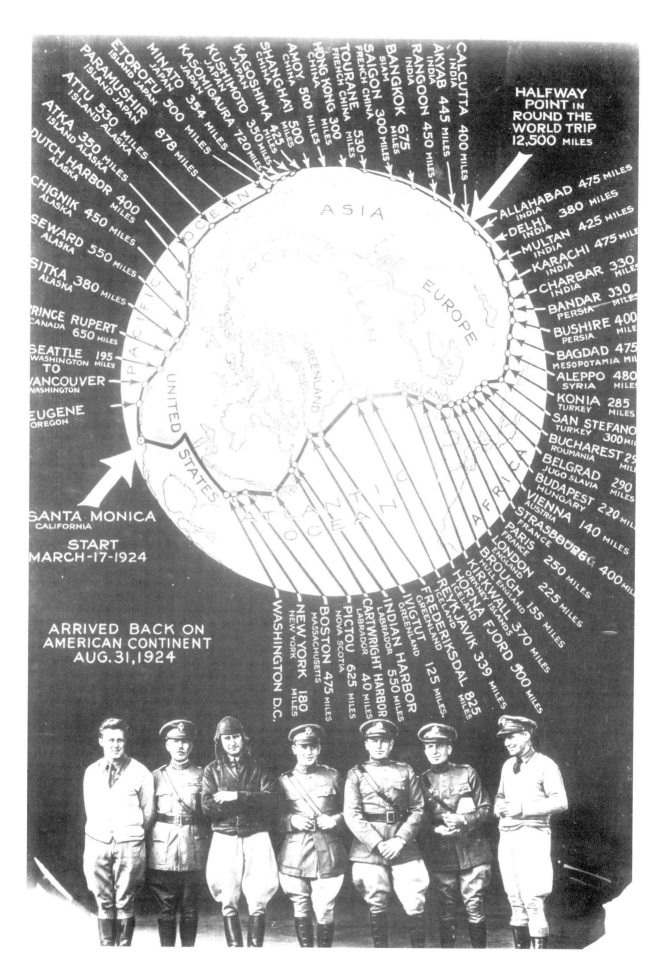

Chapter 1
Planning and Preparation

I t is uncertain who first advanced the idea of sending U. S. Army Air Service pilots on a flight around the world. However, it is known that the thought of such a flight in fixed–wing aircraft first began to form in the minds of a few military pilots as early as 1922. Military pilots, especially the Army's, were being encouraged to bring public attention to the airplane's potential for defense and commercial use by setting speed, endurance, distance and altitude records. A U.S. Navy flight crew had crossed the Atlantic with one stop and two British pilots had crossed it nonstop in 1919; an Army pilot had crossed the nation with one stop in less than a day in 1922; and two Army pilots had crossed the nation nonstop the following year.

Maj. Gen. Mason M. Patrick, Chief of the Air Service, officially endorsed a proposal in early 1923 for a round-the-world flight and appointed a committee of officers to make detailed plans to carry it out. In June 1923, the Adjutant General of the Army authorized travel for two officers of the Air Service to visit the probable routes over the North Pacific and North Atlantic oceans which were believed to be the most difficult legs of such a flight. On December 3, 1923, having received favorable reports that the flight had reasonable chances for success, the War Department approved the Project.

General Patrick, a veteran ground officer who had learned to fly at age 60, felt justified that such an unusual undertaking would give the Air Service valuable experience in long distance flying as well as secure for the United States the honor of being the first country to encircle the world by air.

There was considerable interest at the same time in other countries to make such a flight. British, French, Italian, Portuguese and Argentine airmen were either already attempting the flight or planning for it when General Patrick publicly announced America's intention to make the attempt. There were those who scoffed at the idea because of the great distances involved, the climatic extremes that would be encountered and the difficulties to be expected in the undeveloped countries without aviation facilities that would be traversed.

Gen. Mason Mathews Patrick

General Patrick was in charge of the U.S. Air Service at the time of the world flight. He was born in Lewisburg, West Virginia, the son of a surgeon in the Confederate Army. In 1886 he graduated from West Point and served in the army for the next 31 years. One of his classmates was Gen. John J. Pershing. Patrick served as an instructor at the academy in civil engineering, 1892–95 and 1903–06. He was Chief of Engineering with the army's Cuban Pacification Program and Chief of the U.S. Air Service from 1921 to 1927. He retired in 1927 as a major general. A year before the world flight Patrick learned to fly and met the returning airmen over New York. Throughout his military career he was awarded many U.S. and foreign honors, including the DSM. Patrick died at the age of 79 in 1942.

To counter the doubters, General Patrick insisted that the preparation be the most thorough ever undertaken by the Air Service for a single mission up to that time. Lt. St. Clair Streett was appointed to head a planning committee and four basic decisions were made. Most important, five two-place, open-cockpit, single engine biplanes with interchangeable wheels and floats would be built to Air Service specifications by the Douglas Aircraft Company in Santa Monica, California. One would be a prototype for testing and four would make the flight

Brig. Gen. William "Billy" Mitchell

The father of the modern U.S. Air Force was born in 1879 in Nice, France, of American parents. He was from a prominent family of Milwaukee, Wisconsin. He enlisted in the Army as a private during the Spanish-American War and rose rapidly in the Signal Corps branch, which first controlled the development of aviation in the U.S. Army.

In 1902, he was sent to Alaska to construct a telegraph line through hundreds of miles of trackless wilderness. The experience formulated his idea that Alaska held a prominent place in the defense of the North American continent.

Mitchell learned to fly in 1916 and became air advisor to Gen. John Pershing in World War I. Mitchell commanded several large air units in combat, including the largest concentration of Allied air power during the Battle of the Argonne. He became a brigadier general by the end of the war.

After the war, Mitchell became the leading advocate of an independent air force. He found natural resistance among leaders of the Army and Navy, and appealed to the public through books, magazine articles, newspaper interviews and speeches. Because airplanes were then limited in size and range, many people thought his claims for air power were exaggerated. But he persuaded many others, especially after a 1921 experiment in which he sunk several ships by air attack. He repeated this success twice in later attacks.

But Mitchell failed to achieve his goal, perhaps partly because he was frequently violent in his arguments and bitter in his condemnation of superiors who did not agree with him. He was court-martialed in 1925 for defiance of his superiors and resigned from the Army rather than accept a five-year suspension.

Early in World War II, events confirmed many of Mitchell's predictions. In 1946, congress authorized the Medal of Honor for Mitchell, who had died 10 years before.

U.S. AIR FORCE

---

to improve the likelihood that at least one would succeed.

Second, it was decided that with a departure in the spring of 1924, the safest flight around the world would be to fly westward against the prevailing winds. By going in that direction, they would fly down the Aleutian Islands before the spring fogs, advance through Japan and China ahead of the typhoon season, miss the monsoons in Burma and India, and cross the North Atlantic before the Arctic winter weather began.

Third, the cooperation of other agencies of government would be required to support the attempt. The State Department would be asked to arrange for visas for all the countries where landings would be made. The U.S. Navy and Coast Guard would be asked to provide maps and information on harbors and shore facilities and stand by for search and rescue. American companies in the various countries would be contacted to support the Americans as they passed through their respective overseas areas.

And last, the eight men selected should be the most experienced Air Service airmen available, preferably in long-distance flying. They would have to take training in operating seaplanes and be capable of performing their own maintenance throughout the flight.

On June 24, 1923, the War Department instructed the Air Service to gather data on the Fokker F.V. and the Douglas *Cloudster*, both transports, as candidates for the plane to be selected. Douglas, instead, proposed the planes be based on the DT-2, a Navy torpedo bomber. Delivery of a prototype was promised in 45 days of a receipt of a contract at a price of $23,271. General Patrick approved the proposal for the

Lt. St. Clair Streett

St. Clair Streett was born in Washington, D.C., on Oct. 6, 1893. After graduating from high school, he enlisted in December 1916 as a sergeant in the Signal Corps and was assigned to the Curtiss School in Newport News, Virginia, as a flying cadet. In September 1917 after training in Ohio, he was commissioned a first lieutenant in the Aviation Section of the Signal Officers' Reserve Corps.

In December 1917, he was sent to France and assigned to the Fifth Pursuit Group at St. Remy. Streett served with the American occupation forces in Germany before returning to the United States in August 1919. He was promoted to captain in the Signal Officers' Reserve Corps in November 1918 and received a Regular Army commission as a first lieutenant in the Air Service on July 1, 1920.

His leadership of the New York-to-Nome flight resulted in his being awarded the Distinguished Flying Cross in 1926. After his return to New York in 1920, he was appointed assistant to Brig. Gen. Billy Mitchell, the assistant chief of the Air Service. In July 1922, he became commanding officer of the headquarters detachment at Bolling Field, Washington, D.C.

In January 1924, he was named assistant chief of Airways Section in the Office of the Chief of the Air Service. In September 1925, he entered the Air Service Tactical School at Langley Field, Virginia, graduating the following June. Afterward he was transferred to Selfridge Field, Michigan, and appointed commanding officer of the First Pursuit Group

headquarters. In March 1928, he was assigned to Wright Field, Ohio, as a test pilot and chief of the flying branch.

During World War II, he was deputy chief of the Army Air Force; commander of the Third Air Force, the Second Air Force, the 13th Air Force; and deputy commander of the Continental Air forces (later the Strategic Air Command), of which he was also deputy commander until 1947.

In January 1947, he was made chief of the Military Personnel Procurement Office, and in 1948 was appointed the Air Inspector and later the Deputy Inspector General. His final assignments before retiring in 1952 were as deputy commander of the Air Materiel Command and special assistant to the commanding general of the Air Material Command.

Streett was promoted to brigadier general in 1946 and major general in 1948.

General Streett died on September 29, 1970, leaving his wife Mary, and a son Lt. Col. St. Clair Streett Jr.

U.S. AIR FORCE

Donald W. Douglas

The DWCs were built in the plant of fledgling aircraft manufacturer Donald W. Douglas. He was born in Brooklyn, New York, in 1892. He spent two years at the Naval Academy and then transferred to M.I.T. where he earned a degree in aeronautical engineering. He joined the faculty there and worked on the first efficient wind tunnel in the United States. In 1915 Douglas worked for the Connecticut Aircraft Company which was building the Navy's first dirigible. He next went to work for Glenn Martin in Los Angeles, helping build the Martin Model S seaplane and later the famous Martin bomber. He started his own company in Santa Monica, California, in 1920. It became the Douglas Aircraft Company in 1928 and the McDonnell-Douglas Corporation in 1967. The firm has made many famous commercial aircraft through the years, perhaps the most famous of which was the 1930s DC–3. Douglas died in 1981.

Douglas prototype on August 1, 1923, and a DT-2 on the production line began to be modified to the Air Service specifications.

To be designated Douglas World Cruisers (DWC), they were to be dual-controlled, with the gas capacity increased to 582 gallons for a range of 2,200 miles, have the 12-cylinder water-cooled, 420-hp Liberty engine installed, strengthened wing bracing, and the rear seat for the mechanic moved forward to facilitate communications. Each cockpit would have engine instruments, altimeter, turn-and-bank indicator, drift indicator and compass. One aircraft was to have a radio installed, but this requirement was later canceled.

Sewing cloth onto the wings of a DWC at the Douglas plant.
U.S. AIR FORCE MUSEUM

The wing department of the Douglas plant on Wilshire Boulevard in Santa Monica. Standing in the center is Harry Williams and George Strompl. Williams, with his hands on his hips, was later the superintendent of Douglas' El Segundo plant.
MUSEUM OF FLYING

This was the prototype of the DWC first produced at the Douglas plant in 1923. This plane was later designated the Boston II.
PETER M. BOWERS COLLECTION

The prototype was completed and delivered to McCook Field, Dayton, Ohio, for testing. It was then flown to Langley Field, Virginia, for seaplane trials and crew training. The prototype tests were satisfactory, and Douglas received a production contract for four DWCs at a total price of $192,684, including spare parts.

The course selected was from Sand Point on Lake Washington near Seattle, Washington, through the Aleutians, across the Pacific to Japan, down the China coast, west to India, through the Middle East, across Europe and the Atlantic and back to Seattle via Washington, D. C. The route was divided into seven divisions, and advance officers were selected and assigned to inspect the landing sites in 22 nations and set up facilities for the planes' arrival. Aircraft parts, engines, replacement wheels and pontoons were procured and shipped to appropriate locations.

Lt. St Clair Street, responsible for the route planning, pored over maps and weather charts in Washington while Lt. Clarence Crumrine spent the summer and winter of 1923–24 visiting Greenland, Iceland and the Faeroe Islands for the trans-Atlantic hop. Capt. Lorenzo L. Snow was assigned to make diplomatic arrangements. Lt. Clayton L. Bissell was the advance man for the flight from Seattle to Attu. Lt. Clifford C. Nutt was assigned to arrange for the Japanese stops, while Lt. Malcolm S. Lawton was responsible for the route through China and Southeast Asia to Calcutta, India. Lt. Harold A. Halverson departed to prepare for the segment from there through the Middle East. Maj. Carlyle H. Wash, assistant air attache for aviation in Paris, prepared for the European crossing. Lts. Crumrine, Bissell and Lt. LeClaire D. Schulze made preliminary arrangements across the Atlantic to Boston, and Capt. Burdette S. Wright, the balance of the flight across the U.S. to Seattle. Each man immediately departed for their respective areas. Maj. William R. Blair, an Army Signal Corps meteorologist, began a search for worldwide weather data.

The other departments of government contacted agreed to cooperate. Although the Navy and the Air Service were in vigorous competition for funds and participating in public debates about the future role of the Army Air Service, the Navy did not hesitate to pledge its services as needed. Charts were furnished of the coastal areas where water landings would be made, and ships were assigned to positions where they could patrol the ocean routes and assist in search and rescue. The U.S. Coast Guard also assigned patrol ships along the Aleutians. When the data was accumulated, Streett prepared detailed guidebooks and maps which were shipped to the main supply bases of each division to be available for each crew as they reached them along the 28,000-mile route.

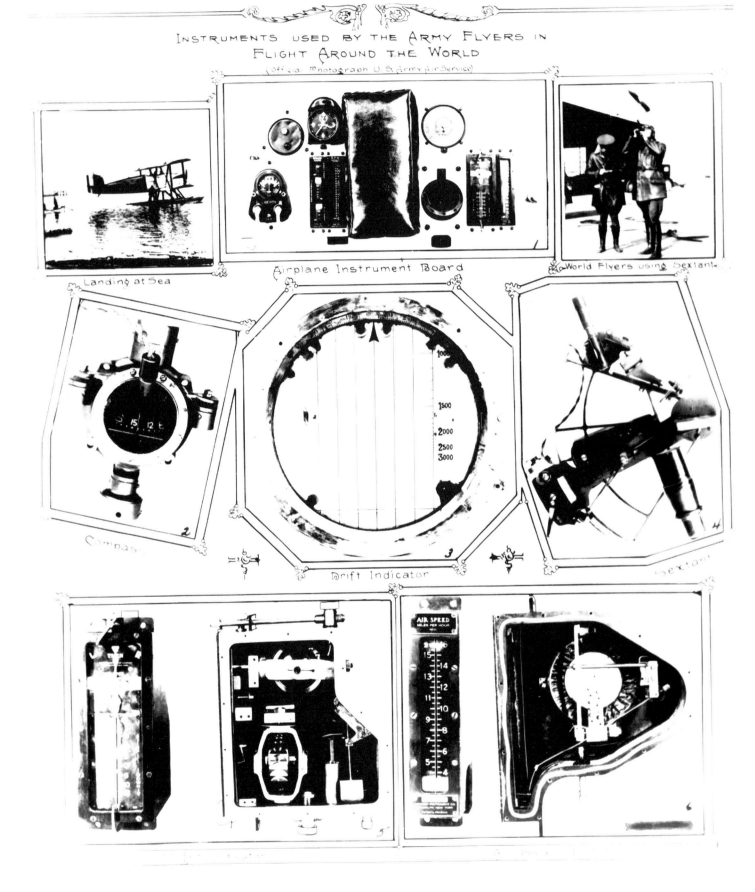

INSTRUMENTS USED BY THE ARMY FLYERS IN
FLIGHT AROUND THE WORLD
(Official Photograph U.S. Army Air Service)

Landing at Sea

Airplane Instrument Board

World Flyers using Sextant

Compass

Drift Indicator

Sextant

Close-ups of DWC aircraft parts.

Liberty engine bed

Aluminum gas tank.

Baggage compartment.

Hand gas pump.

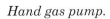

Cutaway view of the improved liberty engine used in the DWC.
MUSEUM OF FLYING

Side view of a DWC at the factory before the insignia, number and name were painted on.
U.S. AIR FORCE MUSEUM

The first of the four DWCs, the Seattle, *is shown here with the workers who built it. This one crashed at Port Moller, Alaska, on April 30, 1924.*
MUSEUM OF FLYING

Front and side views of a DWC with its wings folded back. These give a good idea of the strut system of the biplane.
PETER M. BOWERS COLLECTION

The men selected for the flight gave considerable thought to an appropriate insignia, and several designs were submitted, considered and rejected before the final form was achieved. There was general agreement that the insignia should be emblematic, but it was not until Donald Douglas secured the services of a local artist that the varied ideas of the flight personnel were incorporated into a single, acceptable emblem. The insignia finally selected consisted of a light-blue oval field with scalloped edges. The words "Air Service U.S.A." appeared at the top of this field and "World Flight" at the bottom. The block lettering was in gold. The center consisted of a portion of a globe with the sea a slightly darker blue than the field; North and South America and other land masses, international orange; and the polar areas, white. Two bald eagles in natural colors (brown and white with orange beaks) encircled the globe.
U.S. AIR FORCE MUSEUM

Henry Wetzel and his family with the New Orleans. *Wetzel was a Douglas Company vice-president at this time.*
MUSEUM OF FLYING

These two boys kept a close check on the construction of the DWC. The boy with the goggles is Donald W. Douglas Jr. and his brother is W.E. "Bill" Douglas. Donald Jr. became president and CEO of the company while Bill was a production executive in the missiles division. PETER M. BOWERS COLLECTION

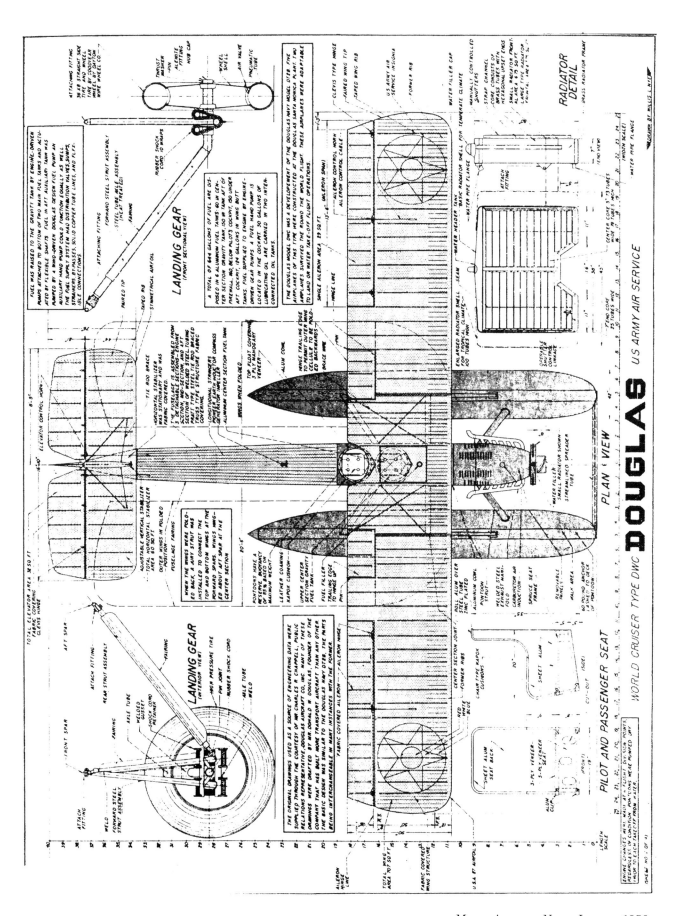

DOUGLAS WORLD CRUISER TYPE DWC — US ARMY AIR SERVICE

PLAN & VIEW

LANDING GEAR (FRONT SECTIONAL VIEW)

LANDING GEAR (INTERIOR VIEW)

PILOT AND PASSENGER SEAT

RADIATOR DETAIL

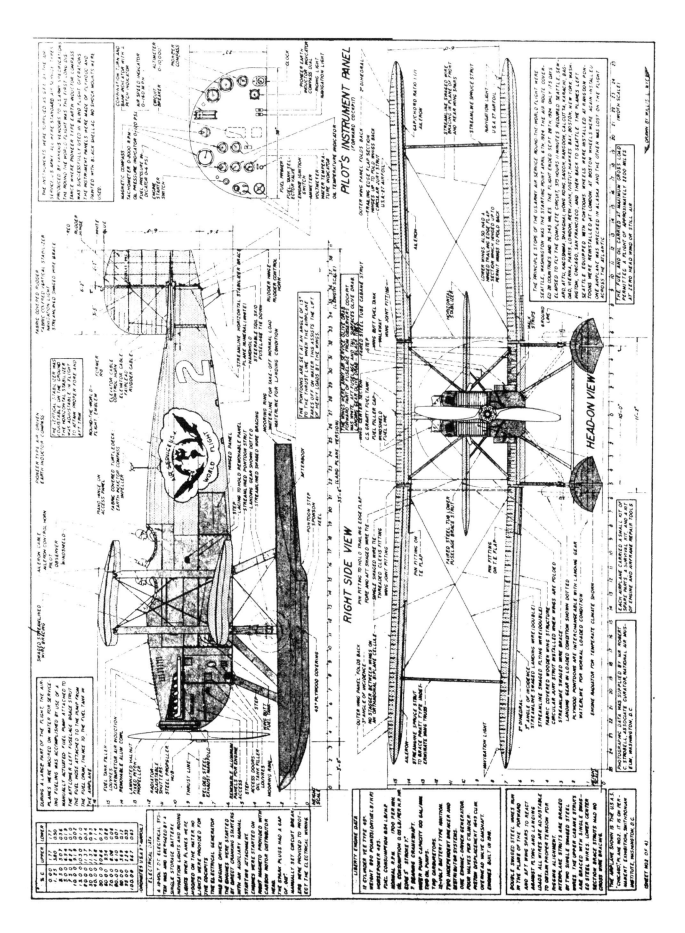

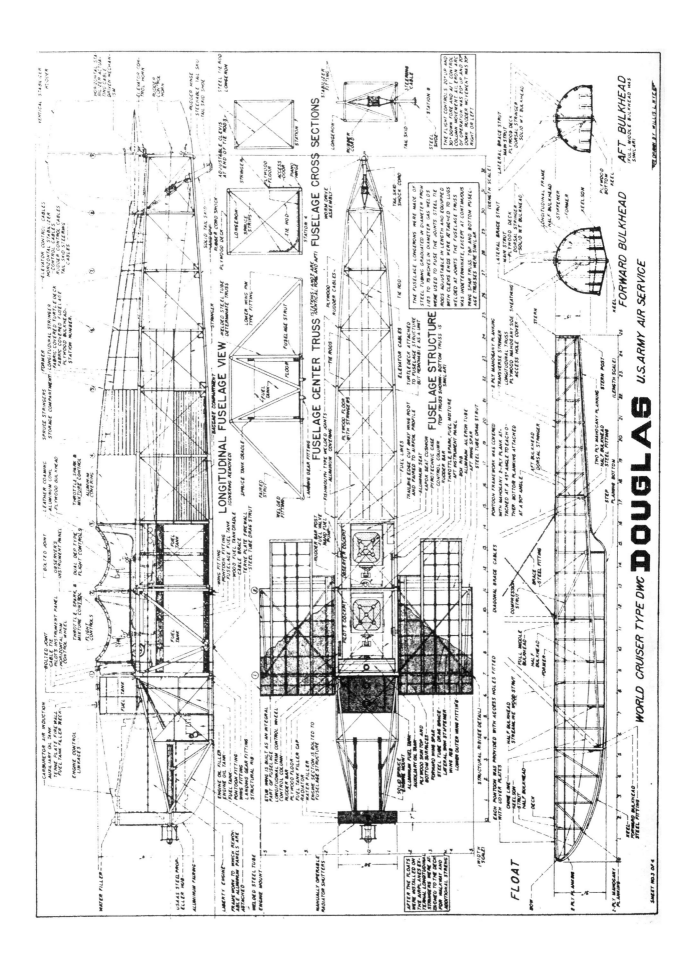

FLOAT

WORLD CRUISER TYPE DWC DOUGLAS U.S. ARMY AIR SERVICE

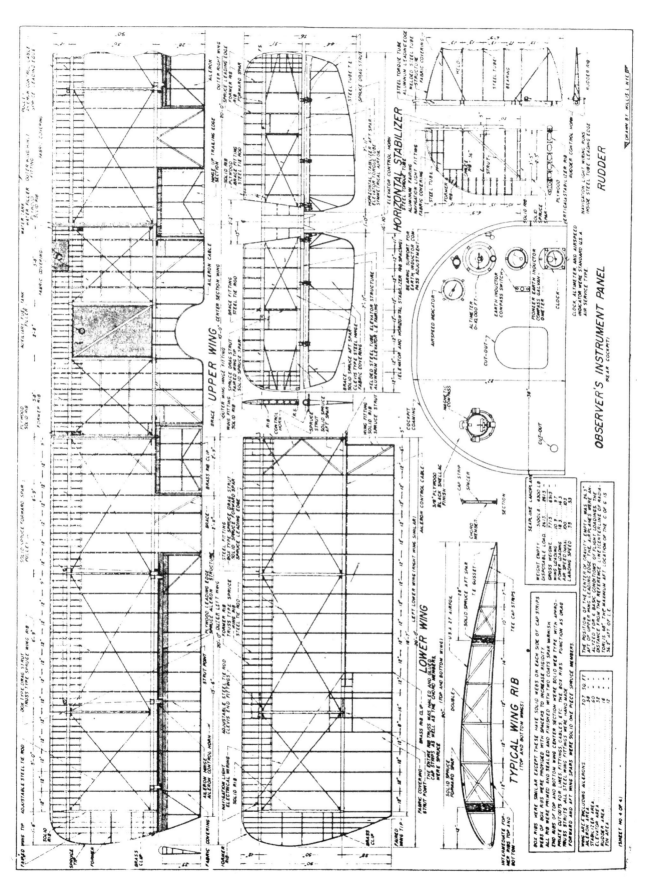

SOURCES FOR DOUGLAS WORLD CRUISER PARTS

Airplane, design and construction — Douglas Co., Santa Monica, California
Engine — the all–American Liberty.

Alemite lubricating system — The Basic Co., Chicago.
Altimeters — Taylor Instrument Co., Rochester, New York.
Batteries, ignition, 8–volt — Willard Storage Battery Co., Cleveland, Ohio.
Batteries, storage, 12–volt — Willard Storage Battery Co., Cleveland.
Batteries, storage, Type A.S.–2, 12–volt — Electric Storage Battery Co., Philadelphia.
Bottles, Thermos — Universal Vacuum — Landers, Frary & Clark, New Britain, Conn.
Breeches, wadding — Goodyear Tire & Rubber Co., Akron, Ohio.
Cameras — Eastman Kodak Co., Rochester, New York.
Coats, Kapok — A.G. Spalding & Bros., New York.
Compasses — General Electric Co., Schenectady, New York.
Compasses, earth inductor — Pioneer Instrument Co., Brooklyn, New York.
Compass, mast — Sperry Gyroscope Co., Brooklyn.
Cores, tire, valve — A. Schrader's Sons, Inc., Brooklyn.
Dope — Titanine Co., Inc., Union County, New Jersey
Ezy–Outs — Cleveland Twist & Drill Co., Cleveland, Ohio.
Fire Extinguishers — Pyrene Mfg. Co., Newark, New Jersey.
Flashlights — Yale Electric Corp., Brooklyn.
Gasket paper, Vellumoid — Fiber Finishing Co., Boston, Massachusetts.
Glue, marine — L.W. Ferdinand &Co., Boston.
Goggles, aviaglass — American Optical Co., Southbridge, Massachusetts.
Goggles, gogglette — E.B. Meyrowitz, Inc., New York.
Grinders, portable — American Grinder Mfg. Co., Milwaukee, Wisconsin.
Hoists, chain — Yale & Towne Mfg. Co., New York.
Hose — B.F. Goodrich Rubber Co., Akron.
Indicators, air speed — Foxboro Co., Inc., Foxboro, Massachusetts.
Indicators, flight — Pioneer Instrument Co., Brooklyn.
Jacks, Badger — Walker Mfg. Co., Racine, Wisconsin.
Lamps, bulbs — Western Electric Co., New York.
Oil — Vacuum Oil Co., New York.
Propellers — Hamilton Mfg. Co., Milwaukee.
Pullers, nail — Bridgeport Hardware Mfg. Co., Bridgeport, Connecticut.
Pumps, bilge — Wilcox, Crittenden Co., Middletown, Connecticut.
Pumps, refueling — Blackmer Rotary Pump Co., Petoskey, Michigan.
Pumps, tire — Frank Rose Mfg. Co., Hastings, Nebraska.
Radiator compound — X Laboratories, New York.
Spark plugs — B.G. Corp., New York.
Spark plugs — Mosler Metal Products corp., Mount Vernon, New York.
Starters, Liberty — Eclipse Machine Co., Hoboken, New Jersey.
Tap and die sets — Greenfield Tap & Die Corp., Greenfield, Massachusetts.
Tape, friction, Dutch brand — Van Cleef Bros. Chicago.
Thermometers, distance type — The Motometer Co., Long Island City, New York.
Tires — Goodyear Tire & Rubber Co., Akron.
Tubes, inner — Ajax Rubber Co., New York.
Unionalls — H.D. Lee Mercantile Co., Chicago.
Valves — Liberty engine — Steel Products Co., Cleveland.
Varnish, Valspar — Valentine & Co., New York.
Veneer — The Haskelite Mfg. Co., New York.
Wheels — Dayton Wire Wheel Co, Dayton, Ohio.
Wires, streamline — Stewart Hartshorne Co., New York.

DOUGLAS WORLD CRUISER

MANUFACTURER   — Douglas Aircraft Company, Inc.
TYPE   — Single-engine tractor, two-place biplane (land or sea)
CONSTRUCTION   — Tubular steel and wood framework with fabric cover. Fittings and cowling are of metal. Floats are of 3-ply veneer and mahogany planking.

Performance

MAXIMUM SPEED	— 104 m.p.h.	100 m.p.h.
CRUISING SPEED	— about 90 m.p.h.	About 85 m.p.h.
LANDING SPEED	— 53 m.p.h.	55 m.p.h.
RATE OF CLIMB	— 53 f.p.m. (approx.)	500 f.p.m. (approx.)
CEILING	— 10,000 feet	7,000 feet
ENDURANCE	— 2,200 miles	1,650 miles

ENGINE   — Liberty V-12, 400-420 hp.
FUEL   — 450 gallons
OIL   — 50 gallons
COOLING   — Water

Weight

WEIGHT EMPTY	— 4,300 pounds	5,100 pounds
WEIGHT LOADED	— 6,915 pounds	7,715 pounds

Dimensions

SPAN   — 50 feet (with wings folded, 20 feet 2 inches)
LENGTH   — 35 feet 6 inches
HEIGHT   — 13 feet 17-$\frac{1}{2}$ inches

Wings

SWEEPBACK   — None
DIHEDRAL   — Upper, 0°; Lower, 2°
STAGGER   — None
GAP   — 110 inches at center section, 85 inches at outer struts
TOTAL AREA   — 707 square feet

DOUGLAS WORLD CRUISER

Upper Wing

SPAN	— 50 feet
CHORD	— 7 feet 6 inches
INCIDENCE	— 3°

Lower Wings

SPAN	— 50 feet
CHORD	— 7 feet 6 inches
INCIDENCE	— 3K

COLOR — From the nose to the back of cockpit the color is aluminum. From abaft rear cockpit to stern the fuselage is painted brown-green, the color being a blend of chocolate-brown and olive-green. Both upper and lower wings, top and bottom surfaces of each, are painted brown-green. The vertical fin is painted brown-green on both sides. All inter-wing and landing gear struts are brown-green. The stabilizer and elevator are painted chrome yellow on the upper surface and brown-green on the lower surface.

MARKINGS — Contemporary star concardes are painted on the right and left sides on the upper surface of the top wing and the lower surface of the bottom wing. On the upper surface of the stabilizer and elevators there are five black radiating lines. These are to guide the navigator in computing drift. The rudder is painted with red, white, and blue vertical stripes, the blue stripe being next to the rudder post. The lettering W-C Douglas is painted on both sides of the rudder as follows: left side: W-C is black, D is white, OUGLAS is black; right side: W-C DOUGLA is black, S is white. The plane's NAME is painted in black on both sides of the engine cowl. A large numeral is painted in white on both sides of the fuselage forward of the stabilizer. Forward of the numeral, on both sides of the fuselage, is painted the insignia of the World Flight. This is a round world showing the Western Hemisphere surrounded by a cloud of light blue–grey. Above the world is lettered in chrome yellow edged with black, AIR SERVICE U.S.A., below the world, WORLD FLIGHT. Two eagles are painted in natural colors on either side of the world, flying toward the center.

Tools and equipment taken on the world flight in each plane.
MUSEUM OF FLIGHT

The original caption simply states, Starlets stowaway in 1924. Apparently some of the airmen attracted the interest of Hollywood movie stars.
MUSEUM OF FLYING

View of the Boston *showing the storage compartment.* U.S.AIR FORCE MUSEUM

The New Orleans. PICTORIAL HISTORIES

Servicing one of the DWCs with pontoons on at Seattle, four days before takeoff. U.S. AIR FORCE MUSEUM

The Chicago *in the Air.*   C.V. GLINES

The Seattle, *with Harding standing on the engine and Martin on a pontoon, is being lowered onto the waters of Lake Washington to get ready for their epic journey.*   PICTORIAL HISTORIES

The personnel were officers and enlisted men recommended by their commanding officers throughout the Air Service. The leader chosen was Major Frederick L. Martin, 42, a Purdue University mechanical engineering graduate, then commanding the Air Service Technical School at Chanute Field, Illinois. Lt. Lowell H. Smith, 32, was recommended by Major Henry H. "Hap" Arnold, commander at Rockwell Field, San Diego, California. Lt. Leigh Wade, 28, who had served in France, was the nominee from Bolling Field, Washington, D.C. The fourth pilot was Lt. Erik H. Nelson, 35, a veteran of the 1920 New York to Nome flight; he was designated engineering officer for the flight. Lts. Leslie P. Arnold and LeClair D. Schulze were named alternate pilots.

Each pilot then selected his mechanic from among ten nominees. Martin chose S/Sgt Alva L. Harvey, 23; Smith selected T/Sgt Arthur Turner; Wade chose S/Sgt Henry H. Ogden, 23, (promoted to second lieutenant during the flight). Authority was obtained to permit Lt. John Harding, 27, a reservist and former enlisted mechanic, to be called to active duty and assigned as Lt. Nelson's mechanic.

The pilots and mechanics reported for duty at Langley Field during the first week of January 1924. There they were given a concentrated study of navigation, meteorology and a course in first aid. The pilots made test flights of the prototype cruiser on floats with various loads up to a total of 8,300 pounds to determine the best type of pontoons and propellers for heavy duty work and to ascertain any weaknesses from extensive use.

In mid-February, the eight members of the flight proceeded to Santa Monica to observe the construction of their planes. The first plane was completed on February 29 and given several test flights by Lt. Nelson who requested a minor change in all the planes to increase stability. The four planes were tested and flown to Rockwell Field where it was found that the Liberty engines in all four had to be changed because they didn't develop sufficient power. The compasses were swung on the Rockwell compass rose and the planes returned to Santa Monica.

Departure of three of the four planes from Santa Monica was made on March 17, 1924, with Sacramento as the destination. Major Martin in Plane No. 1 had a forced land- (cont. page 30)

Maj. Frederick L. Martin

The original commander of the world flight, Maj. Frederick L. Martin was born in 1882 and had been in the army since 1908. He received a mechanical engineering degree from Purdue University and was in the U.S. Air Service in World War One. He became a pilot in 1921 and by 1923 had 700 flying hours. At the time of the world flight he was the commander of the Air Service Technical School at Chanute Field, Illinois. He was selected to command the world flight over future general Carl Spaatz. His time in the Air Corps up until 1941 remains somewhat of a mystery, but there is some thought that because of his several mishaps during the world flight, his flying ability was not highly regarded. However, he was, unfortunately, commander of the Hawaiian Air Force at Hickam Field on December 7, 1941, and relieved of his command along with Admiral Kimmel and General Short soon afterwards. Before the sudden attack, he had advocated a stronger air presence in Hawaii and even suggested that there was a possibility that the Japanese could attack Hawaii by air. After Hawaii, he was put in charge of the Second Air Force in Spokane, Washington, but had to retire as a major general in 1944 due to physical disability. He died in Los Angeles in 1954.

U.S. AIR FORCE MUSEUM

Lt. Lowell H. Smith

Commander of the *Chicago* and eventually commanding officer of the world flight had one of the most interesting careers of any of flight's pilots. He was born in 1892 and graduated from San Fernando College in California. He learned to fly early in his life and for a short time in 1915 flew for the Mexican bandit Pancho Villa. He entered the Air Service in World War One but was confined to the United States as a flying instructor, finally getting to Europe on Armistice Day. After the war he was stationed at Kelly Field and the Rockwell Air Intermediate Depot. From 1919 to 1922 he commanded the 91st Squadron on forest fire patrols in California and in 1919 won a transcontinental air race. With 1500 hours in the air, he was considered one of the best cross-country pilots in the Air Service, a skill that would serve him well in 1924. In 1923 he and his friend First Lt. John Richter established a world flying endurance record of 37 hours 15 minutes, and were the first aviators to refuel in flight successfully. In the 1930s he worked out the procedure for massed airborne landings with George Kenney and piloted the first plane to participate in mass parachuting. During World War Two he commanded Davis-Monthan Field in Tucson, Arizona and was promoted to colonel in 1942. In late 1945 he was killed while horseback riding during a vacation, thus ending a most unusual aviation career.

Lt. Leigh Wade

The commander of the *Boston* was born in Cassoplis, Michigan, in 1897. He served on the Mexican border in 1916 with the North Dakota National Guard and transferred to the Air Service in 1917 after training with the Royal Flying Corps in Canada. In France he was a test pilot, instructor and commander of the 120th Aero Squadron. He continued as a test pilot after the war

and at one time held the world's altitude record in a Martin bomber at 27,000 feet. He took part in General Mitchell's battleship bombing exercise in 1921 but resigned from the army in 1926 to make an oil survey expedition to the Antarctic with Lowell Thomas. The mission, however, did not take place due to the lack of money. In 1926 he became a test pilot for Consolidated Aircraft Co. and later was the company's representative in Latin America. In World War Two he served in Cuba and was air attache to Greece, Brazil and Argentina from 1941 to 1955 when he retired as a major general. For the next ten years he served as assistant to the Chairman and Chief Executive Officer of Kemper Insurance Co. He died in 1991 at the age of 94, survived by his wife Helen.

Lt. Erik H. Nelson

Nelson, pilot of the *New Orleans*, was born in Sweden in 1888 and educated at the Stockholm Technical Institute. He shipped as a seaman, sailing twice around the world. For five years, he sailed under almost every flag in the world. He came to the United States in 1909 and became a citizen in 1914.

He returned to engineering as an automotive mechanic, making one of the first transcontinental auto trips from New York to San Francisco. He then became affiliated with aviation as a mechanic, flying with barnstormers. In World War I, he enlisted as a private and, upon learning to fly, was commissioned. He became a flying instructor and soon was rated the best DH-4 flyer in the Air Service.

Early in 1919, he made a 4,000-mile round trip flight from the Gulf of Mexico to the Pacific Coast, during which he participated in making the first aerial photographs ever taken of the Grand Canyon. That summer, he led a squadron of planes on a 7,000-mile recruiting tour for the Air Service, visiting 32 cities.

Nelson served at McCook Field from 1921 to 1923, and in 1922 he won the two-engine bomber race at Selfridge Field. In 1923, he led a 6,000-mile over-ocean survey flight from Texas to Puerto Rico to Washington, D.C., and return.

In 1924, Nelson participated in the historic Douglas Round-The-World Flight. In preparation for the flight, Nelson was assigned as special consultant to Donald Douglas to help design and build the Douglas World Cruiser used on the flight.

Nelson resigned his commission in 1928 and became a sales manager and later a vice-president and director of The Boeing Company. He was largely responsible for forming the Boeing Air Transport Co., later to become United Air Lines. He also helped develop the Model 247, 40B–4, P–12, F4B, 80–A, and the B–29.

After retiring from Boeing in 1936, he worked as an aviation consultant. During World War II, he worked in aircraft development, especially on the B–29 bomber. He was appointed a brigadier general in October 1945. Nelson died in Hawaii in 1970.

Staff Sgt. Henry H. Ogden

The mechanic on the *Chicago* was born in 1890 in Woodville, Mississippi. He had 5000 flying hours by the time of the world flight. After resigning from the Air Service in 1926, he had a long career in aviation. In 1926 he helped organize the Michigan National Guard and was a commercial test pilot and pilot and manager of the Mazatlan and La Paz Air Mail and Passenger line for the Mexican government in the 1930s. He also organized construction of smelter and mining operations in that country. He designed and manufactured his own small trimotor aircraft, calling it *Ogden Osprey*. In 1939 he moved to England to work for Lockheed Aircraft Corp. and stayed there until 1946. When he retired in 1955 he was a vice-president of Lockheed.

Lt. John "Smiling Jack" Harding Jr.

Erik Nelson's mechanic was born in Nashville, Tennessee, in 1896. He spent his youth on the family's 5,000-acre plantation, attended Webb Preparatory School and two years at Vanderbilt University, majoring in engineering.

He cut his college career short to become a test driver for the Chalmers Motor Car Co. in Detroit and the Dodge Motor Car Co. In 1916 he enlisted in the Aviation Branch of the U.S. Army Signal Corps. He wanted to become a pilot, but never received flight training, so he became an expert mechanic.

In 1919 he was chosen as a crew member of the "round the rim" flight of the Martin Aircraft Company's bomber that flew from Washington, D.C., north to New York and Maine, west across the United States, down the West Coast to San Diego, east to Florida and back to Washington, D.C.

By 1920 Harding was a master electrician and aviation mechanic in the Army but resigned and accepted a civilian job at McCook Field in Dayton, Ohio. While at McCook he became acquainted with Erik Nelson, who selected him for the 1924 flight.

Following the flight, Harding teamed up with the journalist and world traveler Lowell Thomas for a cross-country lecture tour. It was Thomas who dubbed Harding "Smiling Jack." After the tour, Harding worked as a sales representative for the Boeing Aircraft Company and Menasco Manufacturing Co. in Los Angeles, before starting his own company in Dallas, Texas.

As a mechanic and master machinist, Harding always wanted to produce his own product. In 1940 he patented and manufactured his own electric fuel valves. The unit was used almost exclusively on the World War Two multi-engined fighters and bombers. After the war he became semi-retired and concentrated on his land holdings in Texas and California.

Harding died at his home on La Jolla, California, in 1968.

First Lt. Leslie P. Arnold

Alternate pilot and mechanic, First Lt. Leslie Arnold took Tech. Sgt. Arthur Turner's place on the *Chicago*. He was born in 1893 in New Haven, Connecticut, and had worked on submarines in New London, Connecticut, until 1917 when he joined the Air Service. He got to France three days before the end of the war but stayed in Europe until July 1919 with the First Aero Squadron. He served as an aide to Gen. Mitchell during the battleship bombing exercise in 1921. He resigned from the Air Service in 1928 and joined the Maddux interest that later became TAT and Trans World Airlines. In 1940 he became vice-president of Eastern Airlines and served with the Eighth Air Force in Europe during World War Two. He retired as a major general and died in 1962.

Sgt. Alva L. Harvey

Major Martin's mechanic Sgt. Alva Harvey was born in Texas in 1901. He joined the Air Service in 1919, was commissioned in 1926 and retired in 1957 as a colonel. During World War Two he commanded a wing of the 20th Bomber Command in China. After his military retirement, he was a sales manager for a real estate firm in northern Virginia. He died in1992.

One of the official photographs, taken before the flight. Left to right: Harding, Nelson, Wade, Martin, Smith, Arnold and Lt. LeClair Schulze, the alternate pilot who did not participate in the flight. They are wearing a black armbands in memory of ex-president Woodrow Wilson, who had recently passed away. MUSEUM OF FLYING

*Major Frederick L. Martin
and Sergeant Harvey.*

*Lieutenant Erik H. Nelson
and Lieutenant Harding.*

*Lieutenant Lowell H. Smith
and Sergeant Turner.*

*Lieutenant Leigh Wade
and Sergeant Ogden.*

(Lt. Leslie Arnold replaced Sgt. Turner before the flight when Turner became ill.) MUSEUM OF FLYING

Lieut. Lowell Smith

Lieut. Erik Nelson

Lieut. Leigh Wade

Lieut. Arnold

Lieut. Henry H. Ogden

Lieut. Jack Harding, Jr.

World Fliers

Pilots and mechanics. From the left: Turner, who did not participate in the flight; Ogden; Arnold; Wade; Smith; Martin and Harvey. Nelson and Harding are missing. C.V. GLINES VIA U.S. AIR FORCE MUSEUM

Left to right: Mrs. Donald W. Douglas, Donald W. Douglas, Douglas' mother, Major Martin, Lt. Wade and Lt. Smith, at Santa Monica. C.V. GLINES

Pilots and mechanics. Left to right: Martin, Harvey, Smith, Turner (did not make the flight),
Wade, Ogden, Nelson and Harding. MUSEUM OF FLYING

Left to right: Nelson, Wade, Schulze (did not make the flight), Martin, Smith and Arnold.
PICTORIAL HISTORIES

Rockwell Field, a major Air Service base in San Diego, California. U.S. AIR FORCE MUSEUM

ing shortly before reaching Sacramento, California. He was followed down by an escort plane; necessary repairs were made and Martin reached the Sacramento airport later. The three crews proceeded to Eugene, Oregon, then Vancouver Barracks, Washington, and landed at Sand Point, a municipal airport near Seattle, Washington. The fourth plane, piloted by Lt. Nelson, had been delayed at Santa Monica, but he elected to make a nonstop flight the next day from there to Eugene and another nonstop flight to Sand Point, landing there only about two hours after the others had arrived.

The flight remained in Seattle from March 20 to April 6. The wheels were replaced with pontoons and anchors and ropes were attached for mooring. The crews selected the tools and spare parts each plane was to carry and weighed them to assure the total poundage stayed within the 8,300-pound limit for each aircraft. During

this period T/Sgt. Arthur Turner developed a lung condition which disqualified him for flying, and he was replaced by Lt. Leslie P. Arnold, 29, one of the two alternate pilots.

When the day of departure neared, General Patrick issued instructions that the planes were to be christened and named for American cities. Martin's (No. 1) became the *Seattle*, Smith's (No. 2) the *Chicago*, Wade's (No. 3) was named the *Boston*, and Nelson's (No. 4) became the *New Orleans*. They have been referred to by these names ever since.

All appeared to be ready for departure for Prince Rupert, British Columbia, on April 4, but weather reports along the route north were unfavorable. The planes tried the next day, but Major Martin in the *Seattle* was unable to blast his pontoons loose from the friction of the water. The propeller was damaged by the heavy spray and had to be replaced. Seeing the diffi culty, the other pilots did not take off. Thinking the plane was too heavy, Martin and Harvey removed some of their personal belongings from the baggage compartment.

The weather reports showed improvement on the morning of April 6, and the great adventure began. Large crowds gathered on the shore and waved as the *Seattle* made a smooth take-off. The *New Orleans* and *Chicago* followed but this time it was Wade in the *Boston* who could not break the water's friction. He taxied back to the dock, discarded a rifle, an anchor, and some personal items, and departed forty minutes after the others.

One of the DWCs being towed from the Douglas factory to Clover Field for final testing. Notice that the aircraft were built so that their wings could be folded for easy transport. C.V. GLINES

A view of Clover Field in Santa Monica, California. It was named in honor of Lt. Greayer Clover, an American airman from Southern* California who was lost over France in World War One. The field in 1924 was one of 25 in the country established to train United States Air Service Reserve pilots. It is now the municipal airport for the City of Santa Monica and the home of the Museum of Flying. C.V. GLINES VIA U.S. AIR FORCE MUSEUM

Aviation Day
Army Air Service
Round the World Flight
SOUVENIR

Proceeds for the benefit
of Army Relief Fund
Clover Field
Santa Monica
March 16th 1924

Preparations for the world flight at Clover Field, March 16, 1924. MUSEUM OF FLYING

All four planes at the Sand Point Field in Seattle before pontoons replaced their wheels.
PETER M. BOWERS COLLECTION

Christening of the Douglas World Cruisers

The following account of the christening of the four Douglas World Cruisers on Lake Washington at Seattle, Washington, in March 1924 is from the official report of the "First 'Round the World' Flight" by Major F.L. Martin.

At 2:00 p.m. on March 27th, the respective airplanes were christened in compliance with instructions received from the Office of the Chief of Air Service. The christening was attended by the President of the chamber of commerce, Mr. David Whitcomb Jr. and the Mayor of Seattle Mr. Brown. No. 1 was christened *Seattle* by Mrs. David Whitcomb Jr., wife of the President of the Chamber of Commerce. No. 2 was christened *Chicago* by Mrs. Auwilda Connell, wife of Captain Carl Connell of the Air Service. No. 3 was christened *Boston* by Mrs. M.F. Harmon, wife of Major M.F. Harmon of the Air Service, and No. 4 was christened *New Orleans* by Mrs. T.J. Koenig, wife of Lieutenant T.J. Koenig, Air Service. The beverages used for the christening were in accordance with the *spirits* of the times—pure water from Lake Washington, Lake Michigan and the Atlantic Ocean, forwarded from Chicago, New Orleans and Boston, respectively. The occasion was made one of considerable ceremony, each airplane being presented with large quantities of flowers in set pieces and bouquets. The names of the airplanes in block letters, four inches high, were placed on the cowling of the engine, near the nose.

Mrs. T.J. Koenig christens the New Orleans *while members of the air crew look on.*
C.V. GLINES VIA U.S. AIR FORCE MUSEUM

Mrs. David Whitcomb Jr. christens the Seattle *while Major Martin looks on.*
U.S. AIR FORCE MUSEUM

The Chicago *on the barge at Sand Point to repair a hole in one of its pontoons.* C.V. GLINES VIA U.S. AIR FORCE MUSEUM

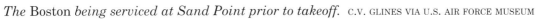

The Boston *being serviced at Sand Point prior to takeoff.* C.V. GLINES VIA U.S. AIR FORCE MUSEUM

FLIERS TO ESTABLISH WORLD AIRWAY!

SEEK HONOR FOR THE U. S. IN AVIATION

Every Detail of Flight Carefully Arranged to Insure Against Mishaps or Failure

GLOBE-GIRDLING RECORDS

	Years	Days	Hours	Minutes	Seconds	Date
Magellan expedition....	2					1519-1522
Philias Fogg..........		80				1872
Nellie Bly............		72	6	11	14	1889-1890
George Francis Train..		67	12	3		1890
Charles Fitzmorris....		60	13	29	42 2-5	1901
Henry Frederick.......		54	7	30		1903
Col. Burnley Campbell.		40	19	30		1907
Andre Jaeger-Schmidt..		39	19	42	37 4-5	1911
John Henry Mears......		35	21	15	4 5	1913

WASHINGTON, March 18.—Will American aviators set a new speed record for circumnavigating the earth on their world-girdling flight?

No. According to Maj. F. L. Martin, in command of the army's expedition, there will be no attempt to beat the records of Nellie Bly, John Henry Mears or Jules Verne's fictitious character, Phileas Fogg.

The expedition, Martin says, expects to return to its starting point, Los Angeles, some time in September, approximately six months after the first "hop off."

Altho the flying time consumed by the army argonauts will be much less than the 24 days required by Mears to establish his globe-circling record, there will be frequent stops for refueling, reconditioning and making repairs.

Aviation experts have figured that the airplane, in its present stage of development, is capable of flying around the world in 300 hours, actual flying time. The aviator, however, would be required to spend much more time than that on the ground between hops.

In a few years they predict, so many refinements will have been added to the airplane that a globe flight will be possible in 10 or 12 days.

Meantime, however, the records of the old-timers appear safe. The breaking up of the Transsiberian railroad has lengthened the route against the attempts of future records along the motoring expeditions and globe trotters.

Alternate Pilots

These men, Lieut. Leslie P. Arnold (top) and Lieut. L. D. Schulze, have been chosen as alternate pilots for the U. S. army's epoch-making flight. If anything happens to the regular pilots, these officers will have to be ready to step into the breach and carry on.

COPS TRY NEW GAS-CLUB

Severyns Says Verdict

A "billy club" that squirts tear gas from the end was given a tryout Monday afternoon in Volunteer park by Chief W. B. Severyns. The test was satisfactory, Severyns said, altho the gas did not shoot out with sufficient force to entirely please the chief.

By a simple twist of the club the gas issues in a stream from the club, becoming a fearsome weapon of defense, but which would not permanently injure a person, merely rendering that person helpless for an hour or so.

"The club might prove dangerous to the policeman using it, however, if the gas came back in his face," Severyns said.

No Naval Base for Singapore; Verdict

LONDON, March 18—The British government has decided not to proceed with the establishment of a naval base at Singapore, it was announced in the house of commons this afternoon.

HERE'S DOPE ON AIR PILOTS WHO WILL MAKE TRIP

MAJ. FREDERICK L. MARTIN—Commanding officer of world flight. Native of Indiana. During World war served in connection with supply. Trained at Bolling, Carlstrom and Kelly fields. Now commanding officer air service technical school, Chanute field, Rantoul, Ill.

LIEUT. ERIK H. NELSON—Engineer officer at McCook field, Dayton, Ohio. Was in famous army flight to Alaska in 1920.

LIEUT. LOWELL H. SMITH—Famous for his part in various refueling-in-flight exploits. Canada to Mexico without a stop was his latest achievement. Native of California.

LIEUT. LEIGH WADE—Native of Michigan. Entered air service in 1917, during war. Trained and served overseas.

LIEUT. LESLIE P. ARNOLD, alternate pilot—Native of Connecticut. Enlisted in aviation service during war. Served as flying instructor. Took special training in aerial photography. Stationed at Bolling field, Washington, D. C.

LIEUT. L. D. SCHULZE, alternate pilot—Native of California. Enlisted in air service during war. Served in France and in Italy as monoplane pursuit flyer. Served as instructor, test pilot and engineer officer.

MIMIC BATTLE

Army Aviators and Cannoneers to Play at Stadium

Details of a sham battle to be staged here in connection with the arrival of the army's round-the-world flyers were worked out Monday evening by Lieut. Col. A. H. Beebe and his staff from the 146th F. A. N. G. W.

The battle will take place at the university stadium on the afternoon of March 29. How co-operation is obtained between flyers and artillery will be demonstrated during the mimic engagement.

Film Accidental Fall of Prince

LONDON, March 18—A motion picture of the accident to the Prince of Wales, in which his horse threw him, causing painful injuries, shows that the prince swerved his mount to avoid striking some spectators, who were crowding onto the course. The horse missed his stride and failed at a fence.

The prince is recovering rapidly.

SLATE REUNION

Seattleites knowing former University of Washington students or faculty members who live in Detroit, Ann Arbor or that vicinity are urged to write them immediately and in form them that a University of Washington dinner will be held at the Union League club, Detroit, on Wednesday evening, March 26. Reservations may be made thru George P. Pierrot, American Day magazine, Detroit.

Among those who will attend are Dean Arthur S. Priest, formerly dean of men at the university, and now traveling secretary of Phi Delta Theta fraternity; Prof. and Mrs. J. Allen Smith, of the faculty of the University of Michigan; Mr. and Mrs. Lee A. White, Mitchell V. Charnley and Mrs. Margery Lindsay Charnley, Andrew Foster, Mrs. Helen Klossman Bryan and others.

These Airmen on Way to Seattle
Will Follow Route Shown on Map in Round-the-World Flight of the U. S. Army's Air Service

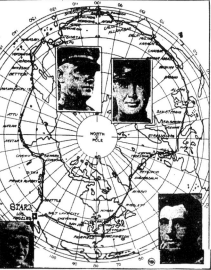

Map of the U. S. army's scheduled globe-circumnavigating flight. The fliers are now en route from Los Angeles to Seattle, where the flight officially begins. Inset are the four designated pilots who will fly the Douglas world cruiser planes on their record flight. Upper left—Lieut. Lowell H. Smith. Upper right—Lieut. Erik H. Nelson. Lower left—Lieut. Leigh Wade. Lower right—Maj. Frederick L. Martin, commander of the expedition.

THEY ARE PATHFINDERS

Uncle Sam has overlooked no bets in making preparations for the army's air voyage around the world. Six officers have been out in the field for months, establishing routes and making arrangements with foreign countries for passage of the American planes. The three shown here have been in the field the longest. Left to right—Lieut. Clifford C. Nutt, Lieut. Clarence E. Crumrine and Lieut. Clayton Bissell. Bissell has charge of the first leg of the flight, Los Angeles to the Aleutian islands.

Here's the Route for the World Air Flight

FIRST DIVISION: Los Angeles, north to San Francisco, 476 miles: north to Seattle, 600 miles, north 650 miles to Prince Rupert, B. C.; northwest 300 miles to Sitka, Alaska; northwest 475 miles to Cordova, Alaska; southwest 156 miles to Seward, and 435 miles to Chisnik; south west 400 miles to Akutan or Dutch Harbor; southwest 380 miles to Nazan, islands of Atka, west 530 miles to Chisgnoff, islands of Attu.

SECOND DIVISION: From Chisgnoff, west 860 miles to Shimushu, Kurile islands, southwest 410 miles to Bettobu, Kurile islands; southwest 410 miles to Aomori, Japan; south 410 miles to Yokohama, Japan; southwest 410 miles to Nagasaki, Japan; northwest 440 miles to Shemuigo, Korean peninsula.

THIRD DIVISION: From Shemuigo, west 350 miles to Tsingtao, China; south 360 miles to Shanghai; southwest 555 miles to Amoy, China; southwest 300 miles to Hongkong; west 500 miles to Haiphong, French Indo-China; south 380 miles to Tourane, Indo-China; south 580 miles to Saigon, Indo-China; northwest 875 miles to Bangkok, Siam, Indo-China; northwest 450 miles to Rangoon, Burma; northwest 443 miles to Akyab, Burma; northwest 400 miles to Calcutta, India.

FOURTH DIVISION: From Calcutta, northwest 475 miles to Allaha bad, India; northwest 380 miles to Delhi, India; northwest 475 miles to Multan, India; southwest 475 miles to Karachi, India; west 330 miles to Chahbar, Persia; northwest 290 miles to Bandar Abbas, Persia; northwest 400 miles to Bushire, Persia; northwest 475 miles to Bagdad, Mesopotamia; northwest 450 miles to Aleppo, Syria; northwest 265 miles to Konia, Turkey; northwest 300 miles to San Stefano.

FIFTH DIVISION: From San Stefano, Turkey; northwest 390 miles to Bucharest, Rumania; west 290 miles to Belgrade, Jugoslavia; north west 340 miles to Vienna; west 400 miles to Strassbourg; west to Paris, to London.

SIXTH DIVISION: From London north 155 miles to Brough, Hull, England; northwest 575 miles to Kirwall, Orkney islands; northwest 275 miles to Thorshavn, Faroe, islands; northwest 290 miles to Hornafjord, Iceland; west 266 miles to Reykjavik, Iceland; northwest 500 miles to Angmagsalik, Greenland; south 500 miles to Ivigtut, Greenland; south west 700 miles to Indian Harbor, Labrador; southwest 525 miles to Mingan, Quebec; southwest 450 miles to Quebec; southwest 175 miles to Montreal; south 400 miles to Keyport, N. J., 290 miles to Washington, D. C., 400 miles to Dayton, Ohio, 840 miles to St. Joseph, Mo., 500 miles to Cheyenne, Wyo., 100 miles to Salt Lake City, 700 miles to Los Angeles.

COASTAL GUARD AIDS FLIGHT

Name Haida and Algonquin to Convoy Big Planes

TO WATCH SEA TRIP

Guard Against Loss of Men on Aleutian Journey

Two coast guard cutters, the Haida, now moored near the Bell at terminal, and the Algonquin, both sailing from Seattle about April 5, will convoy the four giant army world flight planes thru the Aleutian island passage, it was announced Tuesday by those in charge of local arrangements.

The Bering sea patrols will be en route to their summer stations Commanded by Lieut. Comdr. J. F. Hottel and C. M. Gabbit, the two cutters will take with them spare parts and fuel and other supplies for the airplanes, which they will meet in Dutch Harbor, Unalaska, April 15. The cutters will go from Seattle to Seward first to take on extra wings and pontoon cases for emergency use.

On arrival in Dutch Harbor of the planes and cutters, a conference will be held on safety precautions en route to Japan.

Plans formulated here recently by Lieut. Clayton Bissell, in charge of the first division of the flight, and Capt. F. G. Dodge, of the coast guard, call for the following routine thru the Aleutian passage.

One of the two coast guard vessels will sail from Dutch Harbor on a 400-mile journey to Nazan on the Island of Atka. It will radio weather condition reports and any surveys and when those are favorable the planes will hop off with the remaining cutter acting as escort.

The advance cutter will double back and meet its sister ship and the snaumnot haircraft. At Atka one of the cutters will sail ahead to Chisgnoff, on the Island of Attu, then sail for the Bering sea station to Shimushu Island, a distance of 878 miles. One of the two cutters will then sail for the Bering sea station and the other accompany the flight to Bettobu Island, in the Kuriles group, a distance of 495 miles.

Similar procedure will be carried on for the trips from Attu to Shimushu Island, a distance of 878 miles, and from Shimushu to Bettobu where the distance is 410 miles. In the Kurile group, the record ending at Shemuigo, Korean peninsula.

PLANES WILL NOT CARRY RADIO OUTFITS

Lieut. M. R. Lawton has charge of the third division, ending at Calcutta, India; Lieut. H. A. Halverson, the fourth, terminating at San Stefano.

AIRMEN WILL NOT TRY FOR RECORD TIME

Will Be in Air Only 300 Hours, but Stop-Overs and Rests Will Prolong Time of Flight

The round-the-world fliers, now en route from Los Angeles to Seattle, where they will hop off on the first leg of the circumnavigating flight, have three purposes in view in attempting this gigantic feat in the air.

First, it is desired to establish the feasibility of dispatching military airplanes on long-distance flights with satisfactory arrangements of supply problems.

Second, the men will establish a world airway route.

Third, the flight will bring to the United States the honor of being the first country to circle the globe by air.

The expedition is commanded by Major Frederick L. Martin. With him are Lieuts. Lowell H. Smith, Erik H. Nelson and Leigh Wade; Lieut. Leslie P. Arnold and Lieut. L. D. Schulze are alternate pilots. The officers are accompanied by four enlisted men.

In preparing for the epoch-making flight, Maj. Gen. Mason M. Patrick, chief of the air service, has ordered every precaution taken against failure. The proposed airway around the world has been divided into six divisions, each in charge of an advance officer who has covered his section, obtained detailed information and made arrangements for the passage of the flight thru the countries assigned to him.

The first division, from Los Angeles to Attu Island in the Aleutian group, is in charge of Lieut. Clayton Bissell.

Turkey; Maj. Carlisle Walsh, the fifth, ending at London, and Lieut. Clarence Crumrine, the sixth, which brings the aviators back to Los Angeles.

Supplies have been shipped from the United States to various points on the route, and each division has a main depot with one or more subdepots where major items of supply will be allocated.

The planes will have no means of communicating with one another while in flight, equipment being reduced to a minimum for the sake of speed.

The expedition will be unable to take the northern route over Europe and Siberia because the United States has not recognized the soviet government. That means the trip to America is not going to achieve the feat without a battle, for Great Britain and Portugal have been preparing for months and both, it is reported, will outgage some time in April. And France and Italy also are said to be grooming for the flight.

Presentation Address by Miss Marjorie Joesting
Silver Wings to Major Frederick L. Martin Before Around-The-World Flight

Miss Marjorie Joesting Picked for Presentation

A former Alton girl, Miss Marjorie Joesting, now of Washington, D. C., was selected for the formal presentation of a pair of silver pilot wings to Maj. F. L. Martin, commanding officer of the "round the world" flying team which made its getaway a few days ago at Washington, D. C., for a flight around the world. The silver wings had on them an inscription carrying the words uttered by Sir Francis Drake when he started with the British fleet on his round the world trip, "It matters not; God hath yet many things in store for us." A group of officers gave the wings, and Miss Joesting was selected as a friend of one of the officers on the team to make the presentation speech. The actual flight will begin Saturday at Santa Monica, Cal. The party were leaving Washington by train for the west when the presentation by Miss Joesting took place. She is a charming girl, noted for her beauty and is very popular in Washington.

These magic wings carry the high hopes, the confidence, and the affection of your associates and friends. Will you wear them on your round-the-world flight as a symbol of all that we hope for you and expect of you.

Inscribed on them are the immortal words of Sir Francis Drake, another courageous navigator, the first of our race to steer a ship around the world: "It matters not. God hath yet many things in store for us."

It was the unconquerable spirit and leadership, expressed in these words, in the face of storm and mutiny and disaster well nigh overwhelming, that held his crew to their task and inspired them to achieve the impossible.

We have every assurance that our own twentieth century navigators of the air, under your fine leadership, will surmount every obstacle and write their names high on the list of those who, by their vision and achievement, have increased the heritage and sustained the glorious tractions of our race.

AERONAUTICAL CHAMBER OF COMMERCE
OF AMERICA, INC.

501 FIFTH AVENUE, NEW YORK

CABLE ADDRESS "AEROCHAM" N.Y.

TELEPHONE, 3246 VANDERBILT

February 28, 1924.

Captain St. Clair Streett,
Office of Chief of Air Service,
Washington, D.C.

Dear Captain Streett:

Attached please find general list of Ford dealers and distributors on the line of the Round-the-World Flight, as prepared by Mr. Edsel Ford, President of the Ford Motor Car Company and transmitted to us through the courtesy of the Detroit Board of Commerce. The Detroit Board of Commerce advises us that they are requesting Mr. Ford to write a letter of introduction such as you suggested, and this will be transmitted as soon as received.

Yours very truly,

Luther K. Bell

Luther K. Bell.

Apparently, the Ford Motor Company had a hand in the world flight. It is not known if any of these dealers helped in any way.

WAR DEPARTMENT
OFFICE OF THE CHIEF OF AIR SERVICE
WASHINGTON

WGK:hs

March 22, 1924.

SUBJECT: Engines for World Flight.

TO: Major Frederick L. Martin,
            Commanding Officer, World Flight,
            College Club,
                Seattle, Washington.

1.   The report of the Commanding Officer of the Rockwell Air Intermediate Depot upon the condition of the engines which were replaced at Rockwell Field in ships numbers one (1) and two (2) of the World Flight with your indorsement, has been received. In an immediate and personal conference, the Commanding Officer of McCook Field and the civilian engineer in charge of the overhauling of the World Flight engines assured this Office that the engines to be installed in the future are free from the defects reported.

2.   The engines shipped to Santa Monica for installation in the airplanes of the flight were not intended for use outside of the United States. The original plans contemplated flying the airplanes to Washington,D.C., the starting point of the flight. At Seattle, specially overhauled engines were to be installed. These specially overhauled engines are now at Seattle. The four (4) engines intended for original installation were not given complete overhaul, due to the necessity of making early shipment.

3.   The engines which have been shipped to the points on the route have been completely overhauled and this Office has been assured that every change and precaution specified by the World Flight Committee and subsequently by you and your engineering officer, has been made and that McCook Field stands behind the engines which they have overhauled.

4.   Completely overhauled engines are at Yokohama and at all other flight depots; therefore, engines will not be shipped from Rockwell Air Intermediate Depot as you recommend.

By Order of the Chief of Air Service:

W. H. Frank,
Executive.

WESTERN UNION TELEGRAM

NEWCOMB CARLTON, PRESIDENT   GEORGE W. E. ATKINS, FIRST VICE-PRESIDENT

CLASS OF SERVICE	SYMBOL
Telegram	
Day Letter	Blue
Night Message	Nite
Night Letter	N L

If none of these three symbols appears after the check (number of words) this is a telegram. Otherwise its character is indicated by the symbol appearing after the check.

The filing time as shown in the date line on full rate telegrams and day letters, and the time of receipt at destination as shown on all messages, is STANDARD TIME.

RECEIVED AT 341 PLAZA, SAN DIEGO. CALIF. ALWAYS OPEN.

SB505 56

WD NEWYORK NY 15 508P

MAJOR FREDERICK L MARTIN

ROCKWELL FIELD   USA SANDIEGO CALIF

401

MOST ANXIOUS REACH UNDERSTANDING WITH YOU FOR STORY OF FLIGHT UPON COMPLETION APPRECIATE CONDITIONS ENROUTE WHICH YOU POINT OUT HEREBY RENEW OFFER MADE YOU BY MICHELSON IN WASHINGTON OF ONE THOUSAND DOLLARS MINIMUM WITH SEVENTY PERCENT OF ALL PROCEEDS OF WIDE AND VIGOROUS SYNDICATION WILL BE GRATEFUL IF YOU WILL WIRE ACCEPTANCE TO US ATTENTION SWOPE

THE WORLD.

WESTERN UNION TELEGRAM

NEWCOMB CARLTON, PRESIDENT   GEORGE W. E. ATKINS, FIRST VICE-PRESIDENT

CLASS OF SERVICE	SYMBOL
Telegram	
Day Letter	Blue
Night Message	Nite
Night Letter	N L

If none of these three symbols appears after the check (number of words) this is a telegram. Otherwise its character is indicated by the symbol appearing after the check.

RECEIVED AT 113 CHERRY ST., SEATTLE, WASH. ALWAYS OPEN

1924 MAR 22 PM 2 31

NA214 36 GOVT

DI WASHINGTON DC 22 506P

MAJOR F L MARTIN   **1739** College Club

CARE LIEUT T J KOENIG SAND POINT AIRDROOM SEATTLE WASH

PRESS DISPATCHES STATE YOU LEAVE SEATTLE MARCH THIRTIETH PERIOD

INFORM BY WIRE IMMEDIATELY IF YOU CONTEMPLATE LEAVING PRIOR TO APRIL

FIRST IN ORDER THAT ROUTE INFORMATION MAY BE EXPEDITED PERIOD PASSPORT

SENT REGISTERED MAIL TODAY END

PATRICK.

WESTERN UNION TELEGRAM

NEWCOMB CARLTON, PRESIDENT   GEORGE W. E. ATKINS, FIRST VICE-PRESIDENT

A Telegram will BREAK THE ICE for your salesman

CLASS OF SERVICE	SYMBOL
Telegram	
Day Letter	Blue
Night Message	Nite
Night Letter	N L

If none of these three symbols appears after the check (number of words) this is a telegram. Otherwise its character is indicated by the symbol appearing after the check.

RRY ST., SEATTLE, WASH. ALWAYS OPEN

1924 MAR 26 PM 12 40

Fourth Ave. Seattle, Wash

CB310 24 1 EXTRA

Q WASHINGTON DC 26 341P

MAJOR F L MARTIN

COLLEGE CLUB SEATTLE WASH

72

ALL BEST WISHES FOR SUCCESS DO NOT FORGET NATIONAL GEOGRAPHIC

MAGAZINE EXPECTS FULL ACCOUNT OF VOYAGE WITH ALL BEST PHOTOGRAPHS

ON YOUR RETURN

GILBERT GROSVENOR EDITOR.

Aerial view of the Sand Point Field in North Seattle, the beginning and ending point for the great adventure.
U.S. AIR FORCE MUSEUM

The last of the world cruisers the Boston *takes off from Lake Washington on April 6, 1924, for the first leg north to Prince Rupert, British Columbia.*
U.S. AIR FORCE MUSEUM

THE ALASKA DAILY EMPIRE

"ALL THE NEWS ALL THE TIME"

VOL. XXIII., NO. 3520.　　JUNEAU, ALASKA, FRIDAY, APRIL 4, 1924.　　MEMBER OF ASSOCIATED PRESS.　　PRICE TEN CENTS.

GLOBE FLIGHT DELAYED BY STORM

ALASKA BOUND STEAMER ASHORE

ADMIRAL LINE STEAMER GOES ASHORE, STORM

Admiral Rodman Strikes on Point Calvert in Snow—Queen Is Assist

SEATTLE, April 4.—

FORMER POLICE OFFICER, SLAYS

PORTLAND, Ore., April 4.—

Mob Hangs Colored Boy For Killing Police Chief

WOODBURY, Ga., April 4.—

EDITOR PASSES AWAY

NEW YORK, April 4.—

BLACKBIRDS ARE KILLED BY RADIO WAVE, IS BELIEF; HUNDREDS DEAD

BURLINGTON, N. J., April 4.—

Pretty Co-Eds Suing for Re-Instatement

WOMEN GIVEN "JOLLY" TALK BY LONGWORTH

Ohio Representative Declares Republicans Should Be Kept in Power

PHILADELPHIA, Pa., April 4.—

HARTFORD, Conn., April 4.—

AMERICAN GIRL MARRIES JAP FOR RACE TEST

Two Biologists Wed in Illinois After Long Search for Suitable State

DAVENPORT, Iowa, April 4.—

PORTLAND, Me., April 4.—

Socialist Mayor Of Milwaukee Is Re-elected

MILWAUKEE, Wis., April 4.—

1,200 Safely Transferred From Burning Ship at Sea

ALEXANDRA, Egypt, April 4.—

Split Arises Between Mayor and Police Chief

SEATTLE, April 4.—

Five Shots Poured on Miners in Kentucky

PINEVILLE, Ky., April 4.—

Senate Impeachment Court Acquits Official State

OKLAHOMA CITY, April 4.—

FIRE AT HOME

LITERACY TEST LAW URGED BY AMER. LEGION

Alaska Department in Convention at Sitka Adopts Resolution

NAVY PAYMASTER IS DERANGED, IS BELIEF OF WIFE

SAN DIEGO, Cal., April 4.—

ALASKA SALMON IS NOW MOVING

SEATTLE, April 4.—

Gen. Pershing Returns From Long Trip to Europe

NEW YORK, April 4.—

Predicts Recovery of Oil Properties by Government

CHICAGO, Ill., April 4.—

Man Killed, 13 Injured By Tornado in South

DALLAS, Tex., April 4.—

SOUGHT IN GREAT DIAMOND MYSTERY.

WAR SECRETARY IS SUBPOENAED BY COMMITTEE

One Official Testifies He Has Been Suspended Because He Talked to Probers

BULLETIN — WASHINGTON, April 4.—

WASHINGTON, April 4.—

Poincare Threatens Resignation of Cabinet

PARIS, April 4.—

Extreme Pacifism Is Being Extended, Report

INDIANAPOLIS, Ind., April 4.—

Shoots Herself To "Please" Hubby Woman Asserts

TULSA, Okla., April 4.—

SEVERE SHOCK IS RECORDED

Most Violent Earth Tremor Since 1906 Is Registered in California

SANTA CLARA, Cal., April 4.—

DAUGHERTY TALKING AGAIN

CLARKSBURG, W. Va., April 4.—

GLOBE FLIERS HELD BACK BY SITKA STORM

Cloudy Weather Also Reported at Prince Rupert—Fliers Ready for Hop-Off

SEATTLE, April 4.—

DEAD MAN IS AN ARCHDUKE

SAN FRANCISCO, April 4.—

SEATTLE, April 4.—

Stay Out of Politics Is Warning Given Federal Employees

WASHINGTON, April 4.—

INGENIOUS DEVICE IS MADE FOR ATTEMPT TO CONVERSE WITH MARTIANS BY RADIO

CHICAGO, April 4.—

Top: April 5, 1924. Bottom: April 7, 1924.

Chapter 2
Seattle to Chignik

WithMajor Martin leading in the *Seattle,*the *Chicago* and *New Orleans* followed without difficulty . But Martin was unaware that Wade was not following. His view was obscured by several photo planes that pursued them for about the first thirty miles before returning to Seattle. The three planes headed over Puget Sound and Georgia Strait where they ran into fog. They let down to water level and plunged ahead to Queen Charlotte Sound where it became increasingly difficult to estimate their altitude above the water because of the glassy surface. When they reached the open sea, the fog dissipated, but they ran into snow squalls, and the seas beneath them turned rough. At Campania Islands, they avoided snow storms as best they could as they followed the Napean Sound, then through the Ogden Channel to Prince Rupert, British Columbia. The wind increased as they neared the

area, and rain and hail pelted them brutally in their open cockpits. They reached Prince Rupert in a blinding snow storm and landed at 4:55 p.m. They had flown 650 miles in eight hours 10 minutes.

Major Martin leveled off high on the landing, stalled out and dropped about 30 feet. The left pontoon dug into the water, and the impact broke the outer wing struts on the left side. The *Seattle* was hoisted onto nearby shipyard docks to be repaired the next day.

Wade never did see the three planes ahead after he took off and was doing his own navigation where the weather proved to be much better than the others had experienced. He arrived at Prince Rupert only 35 minutes after the others.

The mayor of Prince Rupert met the crews at the dock and greeted them saying, "Gentlemen, you have arrived on the worst day we've

This was the means for getting fuel, engines and supplies to the Aleutian Islands for the four DWCs that were to fly down the chain before breaking into the open North Pacific Ocean.

PETER M. BOWERS COLLECTION

The Seattle's *two outer wing struts, holding the upper and lower wings apart, on the left wing, broke upon landing and four vertical brace lines snapped. The damage was soon fixed.*
MUSEUM OF FLYING

11575 A.S.

ARMY AIRPLANES DO ANOTHER LAP IN WORLD TRIP

Go to Prince Rupert From Seattle, Distance of 650 Miles, in About 8 Hours; But One Minor Mishap.

BAND MEETS GLOBE FLYERS

Next Leg to Sitka, Alaska, May Be Attempted Today; Journey Made at Altitude of 300 Feet; Some Rain.

By the Associated Press.

Prince Rupert, B. C., April 6.—Making the 650-mile flight from Seattle with but one minor accident, the four United States army planes flying around the world arrived here late this afternoon on the first lap of the trip outside of home territory.

Three of the airplanes hopped off from Seattle just before 9 a. m., and arrived here in virtually eight hours. The distance was commanded and led by Major Frederick L. Martin. The plane of Lieutenant Leigh Wade, due to mechanical difficulties, did not leave Seattle until 10:05 a. m., but he made up considerable time, arriving here at 5:26 p. m.

The fliers were met here by a band and crowds of townspeople who gave them a rousing welcome.

Flagship Damaged Slightly.

In landing Major Martin damaged his plane, the flagship Seattle. It is not believed the damage is serious. All the other machines landed safely. Before leaving Seattle today, Major Martin said it was possible the fliers might leave here tomorrow, resuming their flight as far at Sitka, Alaska, a minor supply base, 300 miles from here. In view of the damage to the commander's plane, a hop-off tomorrow was regarded tonight as improbable.

The fliers showed no ill-effect of the flight and were in good spirits. The flight from Seattle was made at an average altitude of 300 feet. Rain was encountered from Vancouver, B. C., to Prince Rupert.

Start of Journey Dramatic.

By the Associated Press.

Seattle, April 6.—A second unofficial report received here from Prince Rupert, B. C., stated that three planes of the United States army on a flight around the world had arrived there at 4:54 o'clock and that a band met the fliers as they came ashore.

The hop-off was dramatic. From the cockpit of his machine, Major Martin waved an adieu to the throng that had gathered to bid him farewell and wish him God speed.

"We are going this time," shouted the flight leader. There was a roar of motors and a cloud of spray. The great mechanical birds soared aloft and in a few minutes were lost in the mist to the north.

Mechanics from an airplane factory here worked all night last night to put the planes in shape for today's get-away. The air officials themselves toiled late and arose early to have everything in readiness.

Lieutenant Leigh Wade, last of the four fliers to leave, hopped off at 10:05 a. m. Too much weight caused his delay and he was forced to leave considerable baggage and gasoline behind him to lighten his plane.

Three DWCs in the harbor at Prince Rupert, British Columbia, first stop on their long journey. Wade in the Boston *was not too far behind the first three aircraft.*

U.S. AIR FORCE MUSEUM

Seal Cove at Prince Rupert with three of the DWCs. It was in this area that the Seattle *had its first mishap.* MUSEUM OF FLYING

The fliers with the mayor of Prince Rupert at the Prince Rupert Hotel on April 8. This would be the first of dozens of receptions at every stop around the world. MUSEUM OF FLYING

The world fliers arriving over Sitka, Alaska, on the Alaska Panhandle, April 11, their first stop in the territory. JIM RUOTSALA VIA SHELDON JACKSON MUSEUM

had in ten years!" That night they were hosted with an official banquet and were presented with welcoming souvenirs and good luck charms, the first of many they would receive in the coming weeks.

Martin had decided that each of the pilots should take turns leading. Smith was designated leader for the next hop to Sitka, Alaska, 282 miles away. It was raining on the morning of April 10, but the weather at Sitka and intermediate points was better, so the four planes took off at 9:25 a.m. They proceeded on a compass course toward Sitka but then had to deviate for many miles because of heavy fog until they reached the southernmost point of Baranof Island. They then followed the coast line into Sitka where they landed in good weather after flying four hours 26 minutes.

It was on the landing that Wade and Ogden nearly had an accident. They happened to get into the propeller wash of the *Chicago,* and barely avoided the rocks on the side of the narrow channel. Wade said, "The propeller wash from another plane is a veritable miniature cy-

clone. It shakes you and throws your ship about and puts you through a series of crazy maneuvers that will turn your hair gray."

The flight departed Sitka on April 13 with a landing planned at Cordova, Alaska, if strong winds prevented a nonstop flight to Seward, Alaska. About 40 miles from Sitka, they encountered snow squalls. The snow became thicker, however, and the visibility was reduced to almost nothing. Erik Nelson describes what it was like:

We had to descend to the edge of the water and crawl along the beach to keep from getting lost. Leigh (Wade) suddenly turned the Boston *sharp to the left as though he had seen a mountain looking up ahead. The rest of us were so close to him that it was all we could do to bank steeply close enough to avoid crashing into each other. By the time we flattened out again, we were separated and out of sight of each other in the snow. But luck was with us, and we got together again in a few minutes.*

The New Orleans *at anchor at Sitka.* JIM RUOTSALA VIA SHELDON JACKSON MUSEUM

The DWCs anchored at Crescent Cove in front of Sitka's Sheldon Jackson School. JIM RUOTSALA VIA SHELDON JACKSON MUSEUM

The planes continued to Yakutat Bay and were forced to fly about ten feet above the breakers which was all they could see.

The beach was covered with snow, and the air around us was filled with it, Nelson recalled. *Everything was one color, and we might almost have been flying in total darkness. Sometimes we flew so low that our pontoons almost dragged on the water. Most of the time I flew standing up in the cockpit, braced against the back of the seat with my feet on the rudder bar so that I could look out over the front of the plane as well as over the side.*

The weather improved, and Smith decided to bypass Cordova. The four planes landed at Seward, a small town that sits in a sheltered arm of Resurrection Bay that furnished good protection for anchoring boats or planes. The crews remained there for two days before departing for Chignik, Alaska, on April 15 with Erik Nelson leading. On several occasions, the *Seattle* was seen to lag behind and then swing towards Portage Bay, but Martin did not signal that he was having any trouble. Everyone thought the major would catch up again, but after about twenty minutes, they all felt that something was wrong. The stiff head winds had taken a toll of their gas consumption. It they turned back to look for Martin and Harvey, the other three planes would run the risk of running out of gas and having to land in strong seas. The three planes continued through fog and snow squalls, and Martin finally caught up with the others. He still did not indicate he was having any trouble, so they plunged on. They flew through Shelikof Strait and again ran into snow squalls. When they emerged this time, the *Seattle* could not be seen. The three planes reached Chignik at 4:25 p.m. after a flight of more than six and a half hours.

Smith, Nelson and Wade hurried ashore in a native boat where Lt. Bissell, the advance officer, had established a radio station, and messages were sent to the U.S. Navy destroyers *Hull* and *Cory,* asking them to start a search. Both ships headed toward Kanatak and Portage Bay and estimated they would reach their areas by next morning. The captain of the *S.S. Star,* an Alaskan mail steamer, also volunteered to begin a search, and broadcasts were sent to all points in the vicinity with a request to look for the plane. Radio messages were also sent to Washington telling of the disappearance of Martin and Harvey, and their plight immediately became front page news.

There was nothing the crews of the three planes could do but wait for information. Martin tells what happened when he and Harvey left the formation:

At 2:40 p.m., after being in the air four hours and thirty minutes, Sgt. Harvey called my attention to the fact that our oil pressure was at zero. This forced us to land with the least possible delay. Fortunately, we were just off Cape Igvak, having passed through Shelikof Strait.

It was necessary to throttle the engine in order to glide within the shelter of Cape Ig-

Residents of Seward, Alaska, greet the world fliers as they arrive in Resurrection Bay on April 13.

Seward Daily Gateway

VOLUME XIX.   NUMBER 89.   SEWARD, ALASKA, MONDAY, APRIL 14, 1924.   PRICE TEN CENTS

Dawes' Reparations Report Says Germany Must Control Ruhr

PARIS, April 12—L. E. Martin, printing the summary of Dawes reparations report said he and associates seemed to have reached their aims and the summary submitted was regarded as authoritative.

The report provided that Germany receive no moratorium; that a temporary concession be made of her railroads; that the industries be mortgaged; that a bureau be established governing the transfer of money from the country insuring the least possible disturbance in the exchange market; the annual payments are to be increased in proportion with Germany's economic recovery; should financial disorders delay or prevent execution of her obligations strict Allied control will automatically go into effect.

Without raising the question of military occupation the report stated that Germany must have full control of customs and state industries such as forests, coal and railroads, in the territory occupied by the French.

PRESIDENT COOLIDGE DRAWS FOR TENNIS MATCH

President Coolidge, representing the United States, drew the first name from the cup for the player to represent the United States in the Davis Cup match.   Foreign envoys were also gathered on the White House lawn to draw names for their respective countries.   This is the first time in the history of the Davis matches that drawings were made in the White House.

Fliers Arrived Yesterday; Will Hop Off Tomorrow

Completing what the air pilots described as one of the most gruelling flights of the trip, the four Army De Haviland planes, Seattle, Boston, New Orleans and Chicago arrived at Seward yesterday afternoon at 3:11 direct from Sitka, dropping gracefully into the water and taxing to their moorings within a few minutes after being sighted.   The long trip of nearly 600 miles from Sitka to Seward in seven hours and 26 minutes, was one of the worst the airmen had experienced on their trip, snow squalls, rain, hail, and tremendous winds causing the intrepid pilots indescribable trouble. Off Malaspina glacier amid the baffling air currents of Mt. St. Elias was found the worst stretch of flying. Lieut. Leigh Wade, commanding the Boston, the flagship of the squadron on the flight from Sitka, said the weather could not have been worse; in fact they did not want to see it any worse, and his comrades voiced the same opinion.

...re because we're here," ...Martin, commander of the ...ot of the Seattle, the ...he airplane fleet, as he ...tisfaction at concluding

...to resume their trip, so complete was every convenience for their refueling.

The planes left Sitka at 7:45, Seward time, arriving in Seward at 3:11. "It was a long, hard trip," said Lieut. Lowell Smith, pilot of the Chicago. "We are sorry not to have stopped at Cordova, but we are behind our schedule and must avoid delays."

The landing of the airplanes at Seward is an epoch in the history of the city. "We were agreeably surprised at the excellence of the harbor and the steady air currents," said Major Martin.

Hundreds of the persons witnessing the arrival of the airships had never seen an airplane other than in the movies, naturally were much interested in them.   To the pioneer and old timer who came into the country in 1898, taking months to make the voyage made in seven hours by the airships, the feat seemed marvelous. Even to the spectator used to airships, there was something fascinating about the closely grouped bunch flying low down and close to the shore line.

The flight from Sitka to Seward was made in sunshine, rain, squalls

California Fruit Bootlegged | **Northwestern Has** | **Senator Reed Declares**

The DWCs beached on Resurrection Bay at Seward.

PETER M. BOWERS
COLLECTION

Major Martin and two Seward residents, walking down the dock toward his plane.

JIM RUOTSALA VIA SHELDON
JACKSON MUSEUM

The Seattle *at Chignik, a small village on the Alaska Peninsula. This would be the aircraft's last stop before it crashed into a mountainside.* C.V. GLINES

One of the perils of flying in the Aleutians was ice, even in mid-April. Here Martin breaks the ice at Kanatak before taking off. JIM RUOTSALA VIA SHELDON JACKSON MUSEUM

vak. The wind was from the northwest, blowing at forty miles an hour. The open sea was rough enough to make landing extremely hazardous, but, behind the shelter of Cape Igvak, the swells were not so high, and it looked as though we could get down safely.

The plane was anchored about a hundred yards offshore, and Harvey found the engine had a large hole in the engine crankcase from which the oil had leaked out. They decided to remain in the plane all night, but it was too cold to sleep. At 5 a.m. they sighted the two destroyers on the horizon and fired three rockets with their Very pistol. The *Hull* approached and sent a launch for the pair of tired airmen. The *Hull* towed the *Seattle* to the village of Kanatak where the entire population of 40 people greeted them. "Upon going ashore we learned that this was the first calm day in eight months," Martin said.

When the word was flashed to Smith and the others at Chignik, Smith radioed Bissell at Dutch Harbor to rush a new engine, gasoline and oil to Martin on the Coast Guard cutter *Haida*. Although the moorings were thought to be safe, one of the planes broke loose that night, and it was decided to beach them for safety. The *Boston* had engine problems and had to have it replaced. The captain of the *Brookdale,* a large freighter, volunteered to help, and the ship's boom lifted the *Boston* from the water onto the dock. The other planes were thoroughly inspected and awaited the arrival of the *Seattle* with their leader. The six world flight crew members were given quarters in the home of a Mr. Strauss for the night.

seas made it difficult to get the engine ashore. Sgt. Harvey and a sailor from the *Algonquin* worked all night in the snow by lantern light and changed the engine. On the morning of April 25, the work was complete, but ice had formed around the plane's pontoons and had to be broken up into pieces and floated down the creek before the plane could be moved to the open

The Boston *was hoisted onto the deck of the S.S. Broodkale at Dutch Harbor for engine repairs.*
-JIM RUOTSALA VIA SHELDON JACKSON MUSEUM

The next day started off calmly, but then the wind of one of the infamous Aleutian *williwaws* rushed down the mountain at from 50 to 75 miles an hour.

After it had blown for a few minutes, another came along from an entirely different direction, Ogden related. *This one picked up big sheets of water and carried them right across the bay. A boat lying on shore went end over end. Arnold and I happened to be walking down the street when we heard a clanking. A big iron drum came bounding along. We jumped out of the way and let it crash into a fence. Then the "willie" hit a pile of lumber on the dock that had recently been unloaded and hadn't yet been lashed down. The boards went sailing off the top of the pile just like a deck of cards.*

Meanwhile, the engine and supplies finally arrived at Kanatak for the *Seattle,* but the rough

BAD WEATHER HOLDS MARTIN AT KANATAK

On Board the U. S. Coast Guard Cutter Algonquin, Kanatak, Alaska, April 21.—Unfavorable weather conditions prevented Major Frederick L. Martin, commanding a flight around the world by four United States army airplanes, from leaving here today for Dutch Harbor, Unalaska, 550 miles southwest, where his three companions arrived last Saturday.

Major Martin's plane, which had a new engine installed here after being forced down during the Seward to Chignick flight, was securely moored and weathering the gale well.

The last view of the Seattle *before she crashed.* JIM RUOTSALA VIA SHELDON JACKSON MUSEUM

Advance officer Clayton Bissell beaching supplies for the fliers in Alaska. PICTORIAL HISTORIES

water of the bay.

Martin opted for a takeoff, despite the ice, and made it. The visibility was poor, and he followed the shore line watching for obstructions on the starboard side of the plane while Harvey watched on the other. Several times they were forced to bank quickly to escape disaster.

Two hours and fifteen minutes passed, Martin reported later, *during which we were far too busy keeping out of trouble to watch the map. But, instead of the storm being local, it seemed as though we were never going to get through into clear weather.*

But they finally emerged into clearing skies over a body of water which they identified as Kujulik Bay, a few miles east of Chignik, where Martin landed. When the storm passed over an hour and a half later, he took off and landed at Chignik in late afternoon.

The pair remained in Chignik until April 30. It was snowing lightly but the wind was calm. Radio reports from Dutch Harbor were favorable, so Martin decided to go on. He was confident that he would soon join the others.

Night scene at Dutch Harbor with planes beached on specially constructed ramps to keep them from being washed out to sea. An unprecedented high tide brought on by a severe storm washed away the ramps, and the planes were saved only after heroic work by the flight personnel and crew of the U.S. Coast Guard cutter Haida. PETER M. BOWERS COLLECTION VIA U.S. AIR FORCE MUSEUM

The three remaining DWCs were beached at Dutch Harbor for protection from the terrible Aleutian weather.
PETER M. BOWERS
COLLECTION

The Boston *on the dock at Dutch Harbor, alongside the* S.S. Brookdale. U.S.AIR FORCE MUSEUM

Martin and Harvey were up early on April 30 and with a favorable weather report from Dutch Harbor, there was no reason to delay further. Martin tells what happened after they took off:

In trying to cross a portage, which was supposed to be low ground, we suddenly saw a mountain looming ahead. I knew this couldn't be right, and, thinking that we might have veered a bit too sharply in leaving Chignik Lagoon, I turned, flew back, took my bearings again, and flew over a level stretch for a short distance until we came to mountains with level ground extending to the northward. Feeling certain that only a slight change of direction could be necessary, I flew north for a short distance. As we were now flying over land, with pontoons instead of wheels, we were getting rather concerned. But blue water was visible to the westward, so we headed for it in an effort to reach the sea again with the least possible delay.

Our ceiling now was about two hundred feet. But somehow that body of water never got any nearer. Instead we were approaching fog. I was now strongly inclined to turn back to Chignik and start all over again by way of the original course. But, as we had come this far and the water seemed near, we kept on. The fog grew so dense that it drove us down within a few feet of the ground. Still, we found no water. But feeling certain that we had left the mountains behind us, I thought it would be safest to climb over the fog, which I felt would sure would only extend for a short distance.

In order to make sure of getting all the way to Dutch Harbor, we had taken on board two hundred gallons of gasoline and oil. With this heavy load she climbed slowly. We had been gaining altitude for several minutes when, suddenly, another mountain loomed up ahead. I caught a glimpse of several dark patches, bare spots where the snow had blown away. A moment later we crashed.

The right pontoon hit first and struck an incline right on the top ledge of a thousand-foot precipice

ARMY PLANES LEAVE ON ANOTHER LEG OF 'ROUND-WORLD TRIP

No Further News Regarding Missing Men; Attu Island Next Stopping Place.

Bremerton, Wash., May 9. — Three United States army planes flying around the earth left Atka island at 10:10 this morning for Attu island, 530 miles to the southwestward, according to a radio dispatch received at the Puget Sound navy yard here.

The flight is expected to take between 7 and 11 hours, the aviators anticipating encountering head winds the entire distance, as the prevailing winds are from the west.

Meanwhile no word was received here today concerning Major Frederick L. Martin, missing commander of the exposition, although the Puget Sound station was in communication with the navy radio station at Cordova, Alaska, which is in daily touch with all the north Pacific ocean, and which reaches to Asia via a station on St. Paul island in the Bering sea.

Relaxation Is Ended.

Attu island, the next stop of the fliers, is the westernmost island of the Aleutians, and is in one of the five groups of the Aleutians, called the Near islands. From Attu the fliers jump to Paramashiru island, Japan, 878 miles away.

The hop-off from Atka island ended a period of complete relaxation in which the three pilots, Lieutenants Lowell H. Smith, acting commander; Erik Nelson and Leigh Wade, and their mechanics had indulged in since their arrival.

where the mountain tapered upward in a gentle slope. The plane came to a final stop about two hundred feet up this grade. The fuselage keeled over on a forty-five-degree angle. The force of the impact drove the right pontoon under the fuselage and jammed it up against the left pontoon. The pontoon struts were splintered and torn loose. The bottom right wing was demolished, and the one above it driven halfway back to the tail.

Two views of the wrecked Seattle *near Port Moller.* PETER M. BOWERS COLLECTION

Sgt. Harvey got out without a scratch, and I escaped with a few minor injuries to my face. But the tragedy to us was that, so far as we two were concerned, the World Flight was at an end.

Martin and Harvey looked over the wreckage and searched out their personal belongings. The wife of the cannery superintendent at Chignik had made them a thermos of coffee and sandwiches which would be their last solid food for several days. From their maps they knew they were on the Bering Sea side of the mountains where there were no villages or canneries. They had to get on the Pacific Ocean side and started hiking in dense fog on a southwesterly course with the help of a small pocket compass. After walking for five hours and with darkness approaching, they realized they were not getting anywhere and retraced their steps back to the plane. They kept a fire going all night with broken wood pieces from the plane and tried to sleep as best they could.

The following day, May 1, the fog was still extremely thick. They had been forewarned that fogs in the Aleutians could last for days. They knew now that rescue efforts would be impossible. Their survival was up to them, so they agreed that they would start for the coast and never return to the plane again.

The fog remained with us for five days, Martin wrote later. *We trudged along, either wading in knee deep snow or slipping and sliding on frozen ice in the higher altitudes. Our only food supply was a quart of concentrated beef which we consumed ateaspoonful at a time in a cup of water. The hours of darkness were short, just four hours; however, the matter of getting any sleep was just out of the question. The little sleep we did get was an occasional short doze while sitting in the snow. No shelter could be found as we were in an area which was totally barren of trees, but we did have a few alder thickets from which we could pick enough dead limbs to build a small fire. The nights were spent huddled in the alder bushes over our small fire that soon melted its way deep into the snow.*

Both men began to suffer from snow blindness. They became exhausted from fatigue, lack of food and sleep but they kept on. Late in the day on May 7, they came upon a small stream and followed it downhill. Later that day the stream led to a large body of water.

They had unknowingly reached Moller Bay, a large body of water that led to the Bering Sea. They followed the coastline for a few miles and found a small vacant cabin whose owner, a trapper, had left for the season.

The two hungry men entered the cabin and found there was no furniture except for a small stove. Some food was found, enough to make biscuits and pancakes, but they found their stomachs had shrunk and they could eat only small portions at a time. The trapper had left a small caliber rifle, and Harvey was able to bag two snowshoe rabbits .

They discovered a label on a condensed milk box addressed to the Port Moller Cannery, so they concluded they were on Moller Bay and that there must be a cannery somewhere in the vicinity. Moller Bay was still a mass of large pieces of ice, and they were afraid the cannery might not yet be occupied for the season. They left the cabin on May 10 in clear weather and walked about 20 miles along the beach. In mid-afternoon, as they rounded a cliff that jutted down to the beach, they spotted a radio mast and smoke coming from the chimney of a building. While they watched happily, a motor launch containing five natives, pulled away from the cannery wharf. Jake Orlon, the man in charge of the launch, saw them and steered through the ice floes to the beach. Martin and Harvey were taken to the cannery where they were greeted warmly by the superintendent and his men.

Radio messages were sent immediately to the War Department in Washington, to the other World Flight members at Dutch Harbor and to the families of Martin and Harvey. The word was flashed to the world that the flight leader and his mechanic had been found and were not injured. They booked passage on one of the steamships operated by a packing company and returned to Seattle.

Meanwhile, the men at Dutch Harbor had problems with their planes. Soon after their arrival, high winds in the harbor drove the planes off their moorings so wooden ramps were built on the beach and the planes dragged up on them and tied down. Each crew worked on their own planes while they waited for word about their leader. It seemed to rain and snow continually and an occasional *williwaw* would roar through the area from different directions unexpectedly.

When there was no work to do on the planes, the men wrote letters, walked around the area and checked on radio reports. Each day they hoped the major would arrive and they could continue. The *Eider*, a Bureau of Fisheries boat, loaded up with supplies for Nazan, the next stop on the flight's itinerary, and departed.

THE ALASKA DAILY EMPIRE

"ALL THE NEWS ALL THE TIME"

VOL. XXIII., NO. 3530. JUNEAU, ALASKA, WEDNESDAY, APRIL 16, 1924. MEMBER OF ASSOCIATED PRESS. PRICE TEN CENTS.

MAJOR MARTIN, ARMY GLOBE FLIER MISSING; LOST ON CHIGNIK FLIGHT

ONLY THREE OF U.S. AIRSHIPS COMPLETE FLIGHT TO CHIGNIK

Navy Destroyers Go Out to Search for Major Martin Who Is Reported Lost.

By The Associated Press.
Cordova, Alaska, April 15.—Two United States navy destroyers, the Corry and Hull, were steaming at full speed ahead tonight for Kialagvik bay, southeast of Cold and Portage bays, Alaska peninsular, to search for Major Frederick Martin, commander of the United States army around-the-world squadron and pilot of air cruiser Seattle, who was believed by three other army aviators landing at Chignik, Alaska late to have been forced down in that district.

Probably Forced Down

By The Associated Press.
Chignik, Alaska, April ... wireless to Cordova, ... Frederick L. Martin ... the United States a ... world flight and p ... cruiser Seattle, w ... been forced down ... Seward today, n ... tion given out ... tenant H. Nel ... New Orleans, ... ary commar ... leaving Se ... three of t ...

Lieuter ...
the bel ... seeking ... southwest of ... Alaska peninsula, ... arof. Mount Alai ... eastern shores of ... Mount Bechara ... Major Martir ... west off ... trance t ... west of Ko ...

NO TRACE OF MAJOR MARTIN FOUND YET; AVIATORS CONTINUE

Will Hop Off Today on Next Leg of Journey Around the World.

By the Associated Press.
Dutch Harbor, Alaska, May ...
While the crew of the revenue Algonquin at Chignik is dire ... search for Major Martin ... mechanic, Staff Sergeant A ... vey, who have been mis ... Wednesday, preparations ... made at Atka Island for a ... morrow morning, weathe ... by the United States arn ... New Orleans, Chicago ... a 630-mile flight to ... Island.

The coast guard c ... here early this mor ... give further assista ... the-world fliers, if ... pected to arrive ... morning. The ... fisheries vessel, ... Atka to Attu, ... when they reac ...

Although throughout the ... Orleans, Chic ... respectively ... II. Smith, ... Wade, cov ... four hour ... from At ... are in ...

Searc ... hope t ... Harve ... level ... forc ... where ...

FEARS FELT FOR SAFETY OF WORLD FLIGHT CHIEF; STARTED FROM CHIGNIK

Not Heard From Since Taking Air on His Way to Dutch Harbor.

False Pass, Unimak Island, April 30.—(By Wireless to Associated Press, via Bremerton, Wash.)—Fears for the safety of Major Frederick L. Martin, commanding a United States army squadron encircling the globe, expressed here today ... a. m. for Dutch Harbor, Una ... Island, and who was not re ... passing any points up to 6 ... tonight.

TOLD WEATHER FAVO...

By the Associated Press.
Cordova, Alaska, ...
Major Frederick L. Ma ... manding a United States ... squadron encircling the ... Chignik, Alaska, late ... bor, Unalaska, for ... o'clock this morning, ...
Major Martin's ... a wireless dispatch ... after receiving th ... reports from th ... coast guard cutt ... tioned at Unga ... between Chign ... bor.

Preparations Completed for More Thorough Hunt.

By The Associated Press.
Seattle, May 8.—A search plane for Major Frederick L. Martin, missing world flight commander of the United States army, will begin at Chignik, Alaska, in about two weeks according to plans revealed here to ... night.
Meanwhile the latest advices in ... dicated that three fliers of the army ... had taken the air from Atka Island in ... the Aleutians today on their ... journey of the Alaska peninsula and ... around the earth.
Plane were declared complete for the ... waters adjacent to the major near of ... United States coast guard cutter Bear of the ... Arctic can be made ready to leave ... Seattle, May ... cisco yesterday ... plane in which the search was ...
That Major Martin would be found was frequently expressed among those of the army, the Navy and the coast guard in the Second district, many of them familiar by long experience with the severity of nature in the north ...

Stories of the crash made headlines around the country.

ALL THE NEWS
EVERY DAY
WORLD OVER

MONTANA'S
"OLD RELIABLE"
NEWSPAPER

THE DAILY MISSOULIAN

VOL. LI. NO. 12.　　　　MISSOULA, MONTANA, MONDAY MORNING, MAY 12, 1924.　　　　PRICE FIVE CENTS.

MAJOR MARTIN AND AIDE ARE SAFE

U. S. GLADENED BY NEWS COMING FROM FAR NORTH

Officials at Washington Say They Never Had Lost Hope That Daring Airmen Would Be Found Alive.

NAVY OFFERS ASSISTANCE

No Instructions to Be Sent Until Condition of Men Is Ascertained; Coolidge Has Been Interested in Flyers.

"A WONDERFUL MOTHER'S DAY FOR ME," DECLARES MOTHER OF U. S. AIRMAN

Still Alive

HAVE MIRACULOUS ESCAPE; HIT PEAK DURING HEAVY FOG

First Word From Them After Tramping for Ten Days to Port Moller, Hundred Miles From Starting Point.

UNDER SEVERE HARDSHIPS

Accident Happened as Aviators Were Endeavoring to Rejoin Other Planes Carrying 'Round-World Flyers.

By the Associated Press.
Cordova, Alaska, May 11.—Miraculously escaping death after crashing against a mountain peak in a fog and completely wrecking the former flagship plane Seattle, one of four United States army globe-circling air cruisers, Major Frederick L. Martin,

Major Martin, commander of the around-the-world flyers, who had been lost for 11 days following his hopoff from Chignik, is safe. He and his mechanician are at Port Moller. They struck a mountain peak during a heavy fog and their plane was wrecked.

Major Martin's wife's sister wrote this letter from Los Angeles upon hearing of her brother-in-laws's accident. It wan an interesting way of trying to speed up the mail service.

NEWS THAT MARTIN IS SAFE RECEIVED WITH JOY BY WIFE

Says She Will Try to Get Him to Promise Never to Fly Again.

By The Associated Press
San Diego, Cal., May 11 —
frozen Arctic was
and sputter of the
radio brought the
erick L. Martin's
here. Her joy at th
of suspense brough
smiles.
"I am going to
me never to fly
declared. "God ble
senger boy that de
gram," she said. "H
sister's house, where
ing since the major
with his face all rad
Instinctively, I knew
me good news."

Cheers at Santa
By The Associat
Santa Monica, Cal.,
longed cheering greeted
ment here today that M
L. Martin and Staff
Harvey, who hopped off
ing field with other the
17, were alive and safe
been practically given u
After the scores of air
gathered here for their
day instruction had giv
their enthusiasm. Lieut
Moseley, commandant of
field, said:
"We're mighty glad to le
major and Harvey are saf
them are admirable fellows and made
hundreds of friends while preparing

Form No. 4 12-23 5m

RADIOGRAM
SHIP OWNERS RADIO SERVICE, INC.
80 WASHINGTON STREET, NEW YORK

....Company

MAY 13　1924

Apparatus owned by..

Received on board S. S.......PORT MOLLER ALASKA.....Radio　Time Rec'd........P....M.　Rec'd by.....G.C.

Prefix....RED....No.......2....Check....59 GOVT.....19.......Time Filed............M.

From.....BELLINGH M WA.....via.....NPQ..
(Office of Origin)

PORT MOLLER ALASKA

THE FOLLOWING MESSAGE JUST RECEIVED FROM WASHINGTON IN OUR CARE QUOTE
107E WE REJOICE AND THANK GOD THAT YOU ARE BOTH SAFE AND WILL CONFIDENCE IN
YOU UNABATED YOU HAVE PROVED YOURSELF STILL WANT YOU TO COMMAND FLIGHT

CANNOT ARRANGE FOR YOU TO OVERTAKE OTHERS BY GOING ON WEST YOU AND SERGEANT

HARVEY WILL REPORT TO ME HERE WITHOUT DELAY PLAN TO SEND YOU EAST TO REJOIN

FLIGHT AT FURTHER CONVENIENT FROM WHICH YOU CAN COMPLETE THE JOURNEY WITH

THE REST OF YOUR COMMAND UNQUOTE PATRICK

DEL'VD TO.............　　　　　　　　PACIFIC AMERICAN FISHERIES

AT.............192....　THIS FORM MUST ACCOMPANY ANY INQUIRY RESPECTING THIS RADIOGRAM

Maj. Martin, left, and Sgt. Harvey just after their arrival at the Port Moller cannery. They had been wandering in snow, sleet and fog for 10 days but came through the ordeal in reasonably good condition. C.V. GLINES

After many days of hiking towards the North Pacific coast, the two airmen found a trapper's hut such as this near Port Moller. Warmth and a little stored food quickly revived the men.
C.V. GLINES

MARTIN ON WAY SOUTH; WANTED IN WASHINGTON

Wrecked Commander of Globe Flyers Gets Instructions to Report as Soon as Possible to Army Officers.

COMRADES MAY FLY TODAY

Forecast for Favorable Climatic Conditions; Planes Put in Tune at Attu for Next Leg of Long Journey.

Martin and Harvey boarded the steamer Catherine D. at Port Moller and arrived at Bellingham, Washington, in late May. Two thousand people cheered them as they disembarked along with Mrs. Martin and their eight–year–old son. This photo shows Harvey being welcomed.
MUSEUM OF FLYING

MARTIN TO COME BACK TO STATES; ABANDONS FLIGHT

Cannery Tender Will Bring 'Round-World-Flight Commander From North; to Leave Plane in Mountains.

COMPANIONS TO CONTINUE

Attempt Will Be Made on Wednesday to Negotiate Next Leg of Journey; to Land on Japanese Island.

By the Associated Press.
Bremerton, Wash., May...

On April 30, they learned that Major Martin had departed Chignik but had not been seen since.

The flight crews spent most of the next two days close to the radio station, and everyone thought the *Seattle* was probably safe in some harbor and had not yet been located. On May 2, a message addressed to Lt. Lowell Smith, the ranking officer, was received from General Patrick in Washington:

DO NOT DELAY LONGER WAITING FOR MAJOR MARTIN TO JOIN YOU STOP SEE EVERYTHING DONE POSSIBLE TO FIND HIM STOP PLANES NUMBER 2, 3 AND 4 TO PROCEED TO JAPAN AT EARLIEST POSSIBLE MOMENT PATRICK

Smith, now the flight leader, immediately told the others to get ready to leave the next day. On May 3rd, the crews were up at daylight, ate breakfast, checked the weather reports down the Aleutian Islands and took off for Nazan on the island of Atka, 365 miles away. They arrived to find that the *Eider*, with Major Blair aboard, had prepared moorings for each of the planes. They landed close to the vessel and when all were secured, the *Eider* left for Attu to establish moorings there and furnish weather reports. The *Haida* arrived at Nazan on May 5 to assist the planes and act as the weather radio contact. They had hoped to have news about Martin and Harvey but they had not been found.

Radio communications were very poor and the *Haida* was unable to contact the *Eider* satisfactorily to assure that it had arrived at Attu until May 7. On May 9, Blair's weather reports were satisfactory and the three planes left at 9 a.m. for the 565-mile flight to the last island in the Aleutian chain. A few snow squalls were encountered, but they landed in the Chicagoff Harbor without difficulty at 3 p.m. to find the *Eider* had again set up excellent moorings. The six fliers spent the next two nights on board the ship.

The *Haida* arrived on the 11th and reported that Martin and Harvey had been found and were safe. The ship's crew assisted in fueling the three planes, and the fliers went ashore to stay in a house owned by a Mr. Schroeder who oversaw the natives. There were only two single beds, so the men took turns sleeping on them.

A severe wind and rain storm came up that lasted for several days, and the *Haida* put to sea to ride it out. The fliers spent the time making arrangements for weather reports and safe moorings for the next hop to Paramushiru in the Kurile Islands in Japanese territory. It was decided to make the flight by way of the Komandorski Islands, landing there only in emergency since it was Russian territory and Russia had not given the flight landing permission. The *Eider*, with Bissell aboard, was to take up station off the shore of Nicholski Bay or to the north, depending on the wind. It was to carry moorings, gasoline and oil. The *Haida* was to take up a location about 50 miles west of Attu and relay weather information to the *Eider*. When favorable weather was received on May 15, (or May 16 when they passed the International Date Line at the 180th meridian), the three planes departed Attu about noon. A half hour later they passed the *Haida*, and saw all hands on deck waving farewell. They circled once in salute and headed southwest.

The remains of the Seattle *were still in place in the 1960s. Souvenir hunters had taken off many pieces through the years. The Liberty engine and a few other parts are now on display at the Alaska Aviation Heritage Museum on Lake Hood in Anchorage.* JIM RUOTSALA VIA SHELDON JACKSON MUSEUM

Chapter 4
First Aerial Crossing
of the Pacific

It had been agreed among the pilots before takeoff from Attu that the three planes would attempt to fly all the way to Paramushiru, Japan, a distance of about 870 miles, if the weather was reasonably clear. They would skirt the Russian-occupied Komandorski Islands which were off-limits because the United States had no diplomatic communications between the two nations. The pilots had been warned that there might be serious international complications if they landed there. However, with the weather so uncertain in that area, it was decided that the *Eider* would lie about five miles offshore in case Smith decided that it would be wiser to land there to await better weather.

As the three planes flew southwestward toward Paramushiru through fog and snow showers, the sky blackened ahead but looked clearer to the west. Smith turned toward the

Komandorskis rather than face what looked like a serious storm. After they changed course, the nearest land was Copper Island, 270 miles away, the most easterly of the Komandorski island group.

This island is nine miles long and one mile wide—not a very large object, Smith said, *and one that could be easily missed in an ocean, had our navigation been at fault. This was our first long over water flight and consequently our first real test, so that, after straining our eyes for hours in an effort to sight Copper Island, it was rather a triumph to see it eventually dead ahead over our radiator caps.*

Smith headed northwest toward Bering Island, the largest island in the group, and saw the village of Nikolski. Five miles off shore was the faithful *Eider*. When the planes came into view, the ship closed to three miles offshore and dropped buoys as Smith and the others circled and landed.

As we taxied toward the buoys, Smith said, *a boat put out from shore, so after mooring we climbed back in our cockpits ready to take off again if necessary. The boat came alongside, with five men on board, two in uniform and three in civilian clothes. Aside from their shaggy beards, they didn't look especially savage, so we climbed down, got into the boats that had come over from the* Eider, *and motioned for them to follow us aboard her. Fortunately, there was a sailor on the* Eider *who was a Lithuanian from Chicago and proved a capable interpreter.*

We explained that we had been forced to put in at their islands because of the storms to the south. When we assured them that we were birds of passage winging our way round the world, and that we merely desired to re-

A Russian boat leaves the Eider *after conferring with the airmen on May 14.*
C.V. GLINES

main overnight, they asked us to stay on board the Eider *and not go ashore. That was exactly what we wanted to do, anyhow, and they knew it. In the meantime, they said they would send a wireless message to Moscow to see what Comrade Trotsky had to say.*

While the fliers waited, the Russians returned to shore and sent out a flagon of vodka to show their good will but the crews were too busy to test it. They refueled the planes from the gas on the *Eider* and got the planes ready to take off early in the morning. At 4:30 a.m. on May 17, just as they were getting ready to leave, the small boat returned with word from Moscow: the Americans must leave immediately.

The flight headed due west in hazy conditions toward the Kamchatka Peninsula and then southward to Paramushiru. The last half of the 585-mile flight was made over fog, under fog and through snow storms. They landed during a wind and rain storm in mid-afternoon and found the U.S. destroyer *John D. Ford* waiting, one of several that had been ordered there as part of the Navy plan to assist the Army fliers. Two Japanese destroyers also stood by; all hands on the three ships waved as the planes landed.

No protected water area was available for anchorage other than the channel between Paramushiru Island and Shimushu Island where the water was subject to strong currents, rip tides and winds. The fliers went aboard the

Ford while the storm continued unabated throughout the night. With the help of its sailors late the next day when the storm abated, the cables tethering the *Boston* and *New Orleans* were replaced with rope because they had nearly worn through from the rough seas banging them around all night.

The Japanese were cordial and had assigned representatives from the navy and army to render any assistance needed. Many telegrams had arrived when the news had spread around the world that the flight had arrived safely in Japanese territory. The following message arrived from John W. Weeks, Secretary of War:

CONGRATULATIONS PERIOD YOURS IS THE HONOR OF BEING THE FIRST TO CROSS THE PACIFIC BY AIR PERIOD THROUGH ITS ARMY AND NAVY OUR COUNTRY HAS THE HONOR OF HAVING LED IN THE CROSSING OF BOTH GREAT OCEANS PERIOD THE ARMY HAS EVERY FAITH IN YOUR ABILITY TO ADD THE CIRCUMNAVIGATION OF THE GLOBE TO ITS ACHIEVEMENTS

The world fliers were the dinner guests on one of the Japanese destroyers but at 2 a.m. they rowed out to check their planes and prepare them for an early takeoff. They left for Hitokappu Bay on Yetorofu Island at 7:10 a.m. on May 19th.

Japanese and American naval officers await the arrival of the world fliers from their long flight from Attu. The man in the black hat is Linton Wells, the Associated Press representative, who followed the flight all the way from the Aleutians to India. PICTORIAL HISTORIES

A fisherman's hut on the shore of Lake Tochimoye, one mile from Hitokappu Bay, the second stop in the Kurile Islands. This was the sleeping quarters for the airmen for several nights. At left is the "inn-keeper." The others are Japanese officials assigned to monitor the British Round the World Flight. U.S. AIR FORCE MUSEUM

The airmen were met with enthusiasm at every stop in Japan. Here the planes are preparing to land with the crowd on shore waving American flags and singing "My Country 'Tis of Thee" in English.
C.V. GLINES

A Vacuum (Mobiloil) Oil Company sign on a Japanese beach welcoming the DWCs.
PETER M. BOWERS COLLECTION

The New Orleans *in a Japanese horbor with Nelson and Harding on the pontoon.*
PETER M. BOWERS COLLECTION

Two of the planes riding out a storm in a Japanese harbor.   PETER M. BOWERS COLLECTION

As they had experienced for many days, the flight was through fog and haze, and as Wade recalled, "one of the coldest flights of the entire trip since leaving Seattle." While the destroyer *Pope* and one Japanese destroyer anchored offshore, the three planes landed on Lake Toshimoye, a fresh water lake a mile inland on Yetorofu Island where they could see several hundred Japanese on shore waving American and Japanese flags.

Heavy fog during the next three days prevented the crews from getting airborne for Minato, so they toured the village like tourists, attended a sumo wrestling match and were served food, "much of it in bottles," according to Wade.

Anxious to continue, the fliers took off on May 22 for Minato at 5:30 a.m. The flight was over many islands, smoking volcanoes and then on top of a cloud bank for more than 80 miles. "Perhaps the most interesting feature of this flight was seeing the villagers rushing out of their huts and running down to the shore to watch us," Wade recalled. "Everyone along the route seemed to know we were coming."

Although they had requested that there should be no reception for them at Minato, an elaborate arrival ceremony had been arranged. About 25,000 people had gathered along the beach with huge welcome signs and reception tents. Giant firecrackers and rockets were set off as the planes taxied to their moorings.

As they debarked from the planes, Lt. Clifford Nutt, the advance officer for the second division, met them accompanied by sampans loaded with gasoline, oil and water; on each was an American interpreter. Since the fliers wanted to reach Tokyo that day, they told Nutt they would not go ashore. "So we gave Cliff the thankless job of expressing our regrets to the governor and committee," Wade said.

The planes were refueled and Smith led the takeoff. The flight followed along the eastern coast of Honshu to Ostura, then proceeded overland to Kasumigaura, a Japanese naval station about 45 miles north of Tokyo. Excellent arrangements had been made by the Japanese to care for the planes, and a crowd of about 15,000 people witnessed the landing, including the Japanese navy's ranking admiral, his staff and American military attachés.

The next eight days were spent changing engines, replacing the old pontoons with new ones and attending elaborate welcoming functions in Tokyo as protocol required. Their regulation Army uniforms had arrived, so they wore them for the first time since leaving Seattle. Everywhere they went, they had a Japanese naval escort and were met by huge crowds. Photographers and reporters besieged them with questions.

While there, the fliers held a meeting with the U.S. Navy officer in command of the destroyer division in Japanese waters. Arrangements were completed for assistance for the next legs of the flight from Tokyo to Calcutta, India. They met Cyrus E. Woods, the American ambassador, and were officially welcomed by the Japanese Imperial Cabinet, statesmen and military leaders. They made an official call on Lt. Gen. Ugaki, the Minister of War, who presented them with ornate silver sake bowls which were given only for feats of courage and endurance. On the bottom of each was engraved a replica of the World Cruiser and an inscription honoring the completion of the first Pacific flight.

The Japanese had more receptions planned, but the fliers had to work on the planes and still had far to go. They left Kasumigaura for Kushimoto early on June 1. They ran into heavy rain and had to fly a compass course for the next two hours since they could not properly identify any landmarks on the ground. When they arrived at Kushimoto, the wind was driving the rain at gale force and the sea was rampaging. Leslie Arnold described what they experienced:

The arrival of one of the DWCs at Lake Kasumigaura, a Japanese Naval Station just 45 miles from Tokyo. PICTORIAL HISTORIES

The airmen put on fresh Air Service uniforms when they arrived in Tokyo for meetings with Japanese and American officials.
U.S. AIR FORCE MUSEUM

Tokyo Imperial University

President's Office   Tokyo May 25, 1924

Officers of the Army Air Service of the United States:

It is a great delight to us that we can welcome you here in our University—you, gentlemen, who have come to our shores across the sea, through the air. All here assembled, the Faculty and members of the Aeronautical Research Institute, cannot but admire your dauntless spirit and congratulate you on the success you have achieved. At the same time we have to envy you, for your daring is backed by science, the exact method and results of its investigations. It is a happy union of courage and knowledge that has gained you your success together with the honor of being the first human beings who have connected the two shores of the Pacific Ocean through the sky, the cold and foggy air of the northern Pacific. The same spirit and skill, I am sure, will soon make you the pioneers of an air trip around the globe.

If one looks back a little, it is your nation that the honor is due of having produced the pioneer aviators, the Wright brothers and Langley, and during the two decades after their first successes in the air the progress of aviation accelerated by your fellow citizens has been simply marvelous. Your indefatigable spirit in conjunction with deliberation and endurance; your success is not merely a result of adventure but a fruit of study and research in the wide and complicated domains of physics, chemistry, mechanics and meteorology.

Gentlemen! Your honor is, of course, a pride of your nation; but the honor and pride are to be shared by the whole of mankind, because they are a manifest expression of [?] and intellectual powers in human stock, —the will, ability, research, means, the methods, all illustrated by your success in man's control over nature.

More than four hundred years ago, slow-sailing vessels carried Christopher Columbus across the Atlantic; two centuries later your pioneers crossed the Rockies on wearied horses and carts; nearly a century and a half elapsed before the two oceans, Pacific and Atlantic, were connected by rail; and now you are going to encircle the earth by your machines high up in the air.

Again I say we admire and envy you. Again I say that your honor is to be shared by the whole of mankind.

March westward, farther and farther to your home! Then start anew toward the west and come again to our shores, and farther to our neighbors and yours through all the continents of the world! Thus through your efforts and successes will the nations of the earth be made closer friends and neighbors.

We bid you god-speed! To the west, east, north and south! We shall everywhere follow your journeys with admiration and congratulation.

Dr. Yoshinao Kozai
President, Tokyo Imperial University

U. S. AROUND-WORLD AIRPLANES ATTRACT ATTENTION OF JAPS

Flyers at Kaumigaura Draw Crowds of Curious From All Sections

By The Associated Press.

Kaumigaura, Japan, May 22.—Three American army airplanes, having flown across the Pacific for the first time in the history of aviation, tonight nestled on the Japan naval flying fields here for a week's breathing spell preparatory to a continuance of their attempt to circumnavigate the globe by air.

Great crowds of curious Japanese from all parts of Japan gathered about the aviation field for a glimpse of the sturdy planes and daring airmen who piloted them from the United States. The visiting aviators arrived here at 5:40 o'clock this afternoon, having made the jump from Hitokappu bay, Yetorofu island, Kuriles—720 miles—in 12 hours and 50 minutes flying time. They made one stop of about two hours at Minato for lunch.

Flyers Will Rest for Week.

The Americans and their planes were in excellent condition upon their arrival, but it has been decided to rest a week here. This will give sufficient time for a thorough overhauling of the aircraft and also permit the United States army officers to pay a visit to Tokio, which is only 50 miles south.

With the landing here today the first and most difficult portion of the around-the-world journey has ended. From Kaumigaura the next jump will be to Kushimoto, 350 miles south at the extremity of the main island. It is a small seaport situated on a rocky irregular coast. Kushimoto is next to the last stopping place in Japan. The aviators will say farewell to Japan at Kagoshima, at the southern end of the southern island of Kyushn.

From Kagoshima the Americans will make their next long water jump of 500 miles to Shanghai.

The sea was kicking up such choppy waves that we flew around half a dozen times before landing, and when we did come down, we bobbed about so that for an hour we were vainly attempting to moor the planes. Lowell ran the motor while I parked myself face down on the left pontoon. One moment we would be near the buoy, and the next moment we would be way off from it. When we got to it again, first it would drop way down, and then the next wave would switch us around and it would be way up above me and I'd be down in the trough of the sea. Time and again the waves broke right over the pontoon, nearly washing me off.

They all finally had to give up and taxied to the lee of a small island but found themselves drifting onto some rocks. They held their planes into the wind with their engines and waited while the *Pope* maneuvered to plant buoys to which the mechanics attached bridles. A boat with a Japanese welcoming committee tried to approach the planes, but the seas were too rough. The fliers spent the night aboard the *Pope* and went ashore the next morning to receive medals and souvenirs. The next day they left in a stiff head wind for Kagoshima, the southernmost city of Japan proper. En route they passed over the *Perry* and *Stewart*, two U.S. destroyers that were patrolling along their route. Wade had to land in a small bay when his engine overheated but quickly refilled the radiator with sea water and rejoined the other two. They covered the 305 miles in four hours 35 minutes and landed in Kagoshima Bay before 20,000 school children. The band on the U.S. repair ship *Black Hawk* played the U.S. national anthem, while the children sang it. "It was one of the most impressive receptions we had anywhere in the world," according to Arnold.

They stayed only one day at Kagoshima, just long enough to allow the destroyers to string out along the route across the juncture of the Yellow and China Seas from Japan to China. On June 4, they planned to get away at daybreak, but the water was so smooth that they found it was almost impossible for the planes to break from the surface because of the water friction. To overcome this, one plane would taxi across the water to make ripples, so the other two could get off. But the *Chicago* had difficulty. The pontoons would not release from the water, and Smith taxied back to the moorings. Smith and Arnold spent the day diving under the pontoons and repairing damage caused when a metal strip had ripped off and made enough resistance to prevent them from getting airborne. When the *New Orleans* and *Boston* circled, Smith signaled them to proceed toward Shanghai, 550 miles away.

These views show some of the crowd of 25,000 Japanese welcoming the world fliers at Kagoshima, the southernmost city in Japan and the last stop in that country. U.S. AIR FORCE MUSEUM

To Mr. John Harding,

It is a pleasure and delight to welcome you at Kasumigaura today. Although yours is not the first attempt to fly around the world, there is no record of any previous attempt having ended in success. We believe, however, after observing your progress so far, that you will attain the goal for which you have set out.

We believe this because we know you possess experience, skill and brave spirits. But before you still lie many difficulties and hardships to be overcome. In meeting these we wish you every success and hope for your safe return to your home.

The Jiji Shimpo feels that your efforts have contributed much to the science of aerial navigation, and in accordance with the regulations of our newspaper we have the honor of presenting to you our medal of honor—a medal conferred by the Jiji Shimpo on those who display exceptional talent and skill and a useful profession.

The Jiji Shimpo

U.S. AVIATORS FOUND PACIFIC FLIGHT FAR FROM PLEASANT TRIP

Lieutenant Smith Says Ten Times Worse Than Fliers Had Expected.

By The Associated Press.

Tokio, May 24.—The great flight of the American around-the-world aviators and the terrible weather which they encountered on their record-breaking trip is vividly described by Lieutenant Lowell H. Smith, the acting commander. "It's been one battle after another," said Smtih. "one continual fight to keep the airplanes from being damaged by the terrific weather through which we have gone. We knew that the transpacific leg would be the worst of our flight. It was ten times worse than we expected.

A portion of the crowd waits for the airmen at Kagoshima.
U.S. AIR FORCE MUSEUM

Chapter 5
China to French Indo-China

An hour after takeoff from Kagoshima for Shanghai, the *New Orleans* and *Boston* passed the *John D. Ford* that was still assigned to monitor their progress. As the crews approached the Chinese mainland, they saw the delta of the Yangtze-Kiang River, one of the largest river systems in the world. The closer they got to the city, they saw literally thousands of junks, sampans and steamers below, all bent on their individual destinations. The harbor master, not knowing how much space the planes would need, had blocked off several miles of water front. The planes landed easily but had difficulty mooring because of the swift tide. They worked until dark tying the planes to the buoys and making sure they were secure, and then they were taken ashore by motor launch where they were met by the chief of the Chinese air force. They were driven to the Astor Hotel, and later that evening the four fliers were whisked to the home of a merchant prince who surprised them with a formal party with all the guests, except the fliers, in evening dress.

The *Chicago* arrived the next day. When Smith saw the crowded conditions on the river, he knew there would be trouble avoiding the sampans on takeoff. He talked with U.S. Navy personnel and asked that they deploy the destroyers farther down the route and prepare an area where they could refuel from one of them. He thought the planes should take off with a light load so as to have a shorter takeoff distance and thus lessen the chance of hitting any sampans. Next morning his concerns were realized. The harbor master was unable to clear a wide path and all three planes narrowly avoided colliding with the river craft.

As planned, the planes landed beside a destroyer at Tchinkoen Bay to refuel after four and a half hours of flight. The water was rough, but all were able to take on the fuel cans and empty them in the wing tanks. The takeoff gave them anxious moments, but they made it and proceeded to Amoy, 250 miles away. They landed in the harbor about three hours later and taxied to the Standard Oil Co. pier. They all worked on their planes until long after dark, then were invited aboard the U. S. destroyer *Preble* for the night.

They did not go into the city on June 7, but as Jack Harding recalled, "The city came to us." Hundreds of Chinese sampans with their curious occupants crowded around the planes, probably the first they had ever seen. The fliers hurried out to their planes, got onto the pontoons and spent an hour trying to keep the inquisitive boatmen from drifting into the wood pontoons and crushing them. The skipper of the *Preble* sent out a fast launch to scare them off but was unsuccessful. He decided to ram one or

Along the China coast the airmen flew past many unusual looking sailing vessels. PICTORIAL HISTORIES

Thousands of Chinese junks greet the world fliers upon their arrival at Shanghai, China. These vessels proved to be a real hindrance when the aircraft tried to take off. PETER M. BOWERS COLLECTION

PART OF U. S. WORLD
AIR SQUADRON LANDS
SAFELY AT SHANGHAI
———
Third of Airships Unable
to Make Journey Due to
Engine Trouble.

The New Orleans *anchored in the bay at Shanghai on June 4.* MUSEUM OF FLIGHT - WADE COLLECTION #SEB-63

One of the DWCs enters the land-locked harbor at Hong Kong. PICTORIAL HISTORIES

two and after a few were capsized by the launch's waves, the boatmen got the message and backed off. Smith decided they should get off immediately. "We had only three hundred and ten miles to make our way down the China coast to Hong Kong," Harding recalled, "so it was not until ten o'clock that we got under way. But we would gladly have said farewell to Amoy at sunrise had it not been for the congested 'aerodrome.'"

The typhoon signals were out when they left Amoy. The barometer dropped with startling suddenness, and the horizon was a solid mass of soot-black clouds through which lightning flickered ominously. They had a tailwind, however, that increased their ground speed to one hundred and fifty miles an hour.

They were only on the edge of the typhoon's path and emerged over a calm sea. However, they then ran into fog and driving rain which seemed a welcome relief with the typhoon behind them.

The three planes arrived over Hong Kong harbor, one of the world's busiest, congested by hundreds of water craft ranging from small dinghies to large warships. The pilots circled a number of times trying to locate the landing area and the small yellow buoys where they were to tie up. They flew low over an American destroyer and received hand signals telling them to land on the other side of the bay where they tied up at the Standard Oil Co. dock.

That afternoon and the following day the crews spent the time refueling their planes and repairing the propellers on all three planes. The *Chicago* was hoisted onto a wharf so the leaks in one of its pontoons could be repaired and a leaking cylinder jacket on the engine welded.

The steamy temperature next morning reminded the crews as they checked the planes that they were approaching the equator. They departed Hong Kong for Haiphong, French Indo-China, and passed Macao, the oldest outpost on the China coast.

On our way to Haiphong, Smith said, *we made a forty-mile hop over a peninsula between the South China Sea and the Gulf of Tonkin. Of course, crossing such a strip of land with pontoons is a rather risky business, because if obliged to make a forced landing you are sure to crack up.*

For only the second time since leaving Seattle, the weather was excellent, and after seven and a half hours, the trio landed in Haiphong harbor where the Vacuum Oil Co. and a U.S. destroyer had made excellent arrangements for their arrival. It was the first stop in French territory, and a boatload of officials came out to welcome them. The crews went aboard the destroyer and the French Governor-General invited them to a formal reception on shore. As the Americans had lightened the loads on their planes for the hop across the Yellow Sea by throwing their excess clothes overboard, they borrowed appropriate items of uniforms from the naval officers.

Smith wanted to get the planes airborne early the next day, hoping to reach Saigon by way of Tourane (later named Da Nang), a 410-mile flight of which 150 miles would be over open sea. But the takeoff was difficult because the river was dead calm. They taxied for ten miles trying to get the pontoons up on the step and break the friction. Finally, all three had to taxi to the mouth of the river where the water rippled enough to enable them to lift off.

Thirty miles off the coast, the *Chicago's* engine began to overheat. Smith turned toward land and sat the plane down in a lagoon. He and Arnold filled the radiator with sea water while the other two planes circled until they saw Smith take off.

For another twenty minutes we passed over wild jungle and rough, unprotected arms of the sea, where there wasn't a hope of getting down without crashing, Smith said. *By now the motor was red hot again and pounding badly, so we were obliged to turn out to sea, all the while scanning the country for some sheltered lagoon where we might come down. As we started to glide toward a lagoon, everything in the motor seemed to be going to pieces, for a connecting rod had broken and poked a hole through the crankcase. I couldn't tell at what moment the ship might catch fire.*

Smith was able to land safely, and as soon as the plane slowed down, Arnold leaped out with a fire extinguisher onto the pontoon in case the engine was burning. It wasn't but the two fliers were stranded in a remote area with no food or drinking water. As the other planes circled, Smith signaled to them that his engine had failed and they weren't going anywhere. Wade and Nelson landed and gave Smith and Arnold drinking water and some food. Nelson and Wade promised to try to get supplies and a new engine to them as soon as possible and took off for Tourane.

There wasn't anything Smith and Arnold could do but wait. Although they thought they were alone, curious natives soon began to venture out from the jungle to investigate, followed by a French missionary who offered no help. Three priests came out later, and Arnold went ashore with them to obtain some wine and food.

Changing the engine at Hue in French Indo-China (later named South Vietnam). Due to locating engines and supplies at strategic locations throughout the world in advance, the airmen could continue on their trip without a delay of weeks or even months. PETER M. BOWERS COLLECTION VIA U.S. AIR FORCE

While Smith waited to keep the native dugouts from ramming into the wooden pontoons, he became so thirsty that he drank some of the water given to him by one of the natives. It was a mistake for which he would pay later.

Meanwhile, Wade and Nelson landed at Tourane and boarded the American destroyer *Hart* that had been waiting for them. There Lt. Malcolm S. Lawton, the advance officer, and the Standard Oil Co. agent figured out that Smith and Arnold had gone down not far from the city of Hue. It was agreed that Wade, Harding and Ogden would wait for a new engine to be brought by a destroyer from Saigon while Nelson would go by automobile with the agent through the jungle to Hue. They bought some food and continued to the river through the jungle until they had to get out and walk in the darkness. They

found two fishermen who said they saw two monsters in the air that afternoon, so they paid a sampan owner to take them up the river. While the natives paddled them, Nelson swept his flashlight around the skies to see if Smith and Arnold might signal back. Eventually they did, and Nelson found the crippled plane and its hungry crew. The three fliers feasted and drank until daybreak.

At dawn, the three fliers went ashore and arranged to have a fleet of sampans tow the *Chicago* 25 miles down the river to Hue. The destroyer *Hart* brought the new engine to Tourane, and while Wade stayed behind to guard the *Boston* and *New Orleans*, Nelson and Ogden and four American sailors loaded the engine on a French lorry driven by a native. They started through the jungle, up a mountain, down into a valley and over a second range of mountains. The truck then had to be transported up stream on a leaky barge poled by seven natives.

When we got to Hue, Ogden said, *we lifted the dud motor up out of the Chicago and then hoisted up the new Liberty 12 and dropped it into place. The whole job took us less than four hours.*

When the *Chicago* was ready, Nelson, Harding and Ogden drove back to Tourane while Smith and Arnold flew there in about forty minutes. The whole episode proved the value of the efficient planning by the advance officers, the unprecedented cooperation of the U.S. Navy, and the skills of the fliers.

On June 16, the trio of planes departed Tourane for Saigon, a 540-mile flight, early in the morning. As before, they had difficulty getting off and had to taxi to the mouth of the river to get some breeze and water rippling for lift-off. The weather was excellent, and they landed

seven hours, 38 minutes later near Saigon in a small tributary stream near the Standard Oil Co. station.

They stayed two nights there and left on June 18. Meanwhile, because of the difficulty in getting off with heavy loads in the hot climate, arrangements were made with a Navy destroyer to refuel at Kampongsong Bay, 300 miles away. The next stop was Bangkok, Siam, another 300-mile flight.

Landings were made in the Bangkok River at about 4:15 p.m. June 19. The water was full of floating logs and debris, and the current was very swift. As the official report notes, "No special difficulty was encountered, except in keeping boats a sufficient distance away to avoid hitting the planes. For this purpose, native police were used, as well as sailors from the U. S. destroyer standing in the harbor."

Smith decided to fly directly across the Malay Peninsula en route to Rangoon, Burma, so the crews delayed one day in Bangkok to allow the destroyer escort to steam around the peninsula into Tavoy Bay in Burma where a temporary refueling base had been established. They toured the city, visited Buddha temples and returned to the destroyer that evening.

On the way up the Mekong River and across the jungles of Indo-China to Siam. PICTORIAL HISTORIES

Chapter 6
Bangkok to Calcutta

Lowell Smith, as the flight commander, had a choice to make on the route from Bangkok to Tavoy, Burma. They could go around the Malay Peninsula or fly over it. If they went around and across the Gulf of Siam and the South China Sea to Singapore near the Equator and then to Tavoy, the flight would be nearly 1,000 miles. If they flew on a direct course over the humid jungles of the peninsula where a forced landing would be disastrous, the flight would be shortened by over 800 miles. Smith decided to take the short cut.

The pilots experienced the same difficulty as before taking the heavy planes off from the Menam River at Bangkok—a glassy water surface river and heavy boat traffic. But they departed safely and headed over dense jungle out of gliding distance from any water. The clouds were low, and in passing over a ridge of 4,000-ft. mountains, the *New Orleans* was caught in a severe down draft. When Nelson saw that he couldn't clear the mountain top, he made a 180-degree turn and tried a second time but still couldn't persuade the Cruiser to rise high enough.

Meanwhile, the other planes flew back and circled. "At last we made the ridge," Jack Harding recalled, "and I'll say we were the happiest airmen east of the Suez when we finally succeeded in climbing out of the pocket and winding through the mountains until we reached the sea."

The flight landed at Tavoy where the destroyer *Sicard* was waiting with fuel. Before the planes finished refueling, a storm came up from the south making the water exceedingly dangerous for the planes to remain. Although the weather en route to Rangoon, the next stop, was marginal, Smith decided they should get airborne as soon as possible. In trying to get into the air, the *New Orleans* had several of its vertical wing wires snapped and had to land to have them fixed before they could continue.

Wade in the *Boston* also had broken wires but continued with the wires dangling in the air. The *Chicago* lifted off, and rather than make a dangerous landing to assist Nelson, Smith and Wade continued to Rangoon and landed at a commercial seaplane station on the Irrawaddy River in late afternoon. The *New Orleans* arrived about a half hour later.

When the planes arrived at their moorings near an old British army camp north of the city, it was found the buoys had been placed too close together and had to be moved, a dangerous operation because of the swift river current. While trying to tie up at one of them, Arnold fell into the water, and Smith had a difficult time maneuvering the plane so Arnold could get back on the pontoons.

When the planes were safely moored, the crews were welcomed to Burma by local dignitaries with a dinner and met British army officers who were stationed nearby. Although a guard was moored around the planes, a heavily loaded native sampan smashed into the *New Orleans* and seriously damaged a wing. It was hauled ashore, and it took three days to make repairs by a seaplane company while the men remained in town.

The flight plan called for a wait of one day to allow an escort destroyer time to get to Akyab. It was just as well because Smith became seriously ill with dysentery, a result of drinking water furnished by natives when he was forced down near Hue. He received excellent medical attention from British doctors and was well enough to continue the flight three days later. They departed on the morning of June 25.

The route to Akyab, Burma, 480 miles away, was over a large number of canals and rivers on the Pegu Peninsula, so the flight took an overland course. Although the route was easy to follow, the three planes experienced typhoon weather that was unnerving because of its fury, and they flew out to sea briefly to escape the

An aerial view of Rangoon, Burma, the next stop after leaving Bangkok, Siam. MUSEUM OF FLYING

worst of it. During this flight, they passed over the British flyer A. S. MacLaren who was flying in the opposite direction in his attempt to fly around the globe. He had landed in an protected harbor to escape the typhoon that the Americans were flying through.

They emerged in poor visibility and rain at Akyab Harbor and circled for landing, but Smith decided not to use the moorings set up by the advance officer and instead tied up to those placed by the *Sicard*. This was to take advantage of being near the destroyer that could use its searchlights at night to see if natives were disturbing the planes.

They remained overnight and departed early in a heavy rain storm on June 26 for Chittagong, Burma, to try to get ahead of the severe typhoon weather. They plunged ahead through the rain for the 180-mile flight which was mostly over

The world airmen pass by the gold and jewelled spine of Shwe Dagon on their way from Rangoon to Hindustan. PICTORIAL HISTORIES

swamps and jungle. "As we approached the Bay of Bengal," Smith reported, "we encountered one of the heaviest rainstorms in our experience, the water lashing our faces and pouring in behind our goggles. We attempted to fly around it, but were unable to find any break in it."

They reached the other side of the storm and landed in the wide Chittagong River where the U.S. destroyer *Preston* had set up excellent refueling operations. The flight left shortly after noon for Calcutta and took a direct compass course over a dangerous stretch of jungle and swamp for Port Canning, 25 miles north of Calcutta, and then followed the railroad up the river where moorings had been established. Drenched with perspiration from the stifling heat, they were taken by the British commissioner's launch to the Great Eastern Hotel in Calcutta.

Calcutta was an important milestone in the flight for it was here that the ponderous pontoons were to be exchanged for wheels. The planes were towed to a dock by a motor launch from one of the destroyers, and a large crane hoisted them up so the pontoons could be removed and the wheels attached. The planes were then rolled to the Maidan, a large park near the center of Calcutta which proved to be an excellent field for aircraft operations where supplies and spare parts had been accumulated there as planned.

Much work had to be done on the planes, including engine changes. The planes were pushed into the shade of a grove of trees and overhauled. The monsoon season was approaching rapidly, and the fliers were anxious to get away as soon as possible. The six airmen worked until long after dark for several days. Hundreds of Indians gathered to watch the Americans, and it took fifty policemen to hold them away from the planes. A call for volunteers from the destroyers resulted in many sailors arriving who wanted the opportunity to help on a flight that was getting world attention.

However, the tired airmen did take some time off to see the sights of one of the world's most crowded cities. They went shopping, had their laundry done and had uniforms made. They were treated to tours of the area and saw "the sacred cows that wander around the streets and houses at will, the goats and children that are everywhere, and the monkeys that are as

Up the sacred Ganges past the jute mills of the second city of the British Empire. PICTORIAL HISTORIES

common as birds at home," as Arnold noted in his diary.

Smith declared they would depart on July 1, but the evening before he stepped into a hole en route to a dinner party and broke a rib. He was taped up and obviously in pain but said they would still depart the next day.

The three planes took off early on the morning of July 1 for Allahabad, India, and were surprised by how light and responsive the planes felt with the wheels attached instead of the pontoons. But there were now seven men in the three planes. Linton O. Wells, an adventurous Associated Press reporter based in Tokyo, had been following the flight's progress and wired frequent stories about it to his office in the States after they left Seattle. He had managed to get to Calcutta and was supposed to return to Tokyo when the fliers left for the next leg. He wanted to continue and when he found that the planes were now much lighter without the one-thousand-pound pontoons, he thought an additional weight of 140 pounds would make very little difference in the performance of the Cruis-

ers. He asked to continue aboard one of them across the Middle East and Europe. He had been a big help while the planes were being readied for this leg of the flight and the fliers liked him. Smith sent a message to Washington asking for permission to take him along. When no reply was received by the time they were to depart from Calcutta, Wade let him crowd in with Henry Ogden in the rear seat of the *Boston*. The two were extremely uncomfortable, and Ogden was not happy with the arrangement as the plane plunged through blowing sand storms and stifling heat. Despite what has been reported ever since, Wells was not a stowaway.

The flight to Allahabad took six and a half hours, mostly in clear but very hot weather with a few showers. They landed at a Royal Air Force field at Allahabad, were met by British officers, had dinner at their club and stayed there overnight while British soldiers guarded their planes. Next morning the Cruisers departed for Ambala, a 480-mile flight, passing over Campore and Delhi and landed at the RAF base used for operations along the Indian frontier. The *New*

At Calcutta the three remaining DWCs were overhauled and wheels replaced the pontoons for the next phase of the trip across Asia and Europe to Britain. The Royal Air Force facilities in India were a tremendous help in servicing the aircraft. U.S. AIR FORCE MUSEUM

Allahabad, northwest of Calcutta, was the next service point for the DWCs. C.V. GLINES

Orleans developed a leak in a cylinder jacket, and as the British had a major repair and supply depot at Lahore where they maintained a stock of Liberty engines and parts, they agreed to send a new cylinder to Ambala. Nelson and Harding installed it the next day, and the flight continued to Multan, India, July 3.

The route of flight was along the edge of the Sind Desert through a sand storm which blasted them unmercifully and cut down the visibility to a few yards. They followed a railroad but had to fly low in order to see it and the heat singed their faces. The sand was so fine that it sifted through their clothes and filled their eyes, ears, noses and mouths. They landed on the parade ground at Multan and were told that the city was the hottest place in India. During the day the temperature averaged a steamy 116 degrees with a low average at night of 98.

The crews were given quarters at the British base, washed the sand off their bodies and dined at the regimental mess. None of them slept well, and, anxious to escape the daytime heat, they departed at 6 a.m. next morning for Karachi.

The next leg of the flight went well until the engine of the *New Orleans* began to run rough. The others could see white puffs of smoke pouring from the ship and oil running down the fuselage. It was open desert down below, but Nelson signaled that he was going to fly about 30 miles to the east where he knew there was a railroad. He would follow it to Karachi so he would be near it as a line of communication if he had to land. As he turned, pieces of metal began to fly out the engine exhaust stacks and through the engine cowling. One of the chunks of metal tore a hole in the wing fabric; another hit a wing strut. A piece of metal grazed Harding's temple as both men looked for a safe place to land.

Nelson throttled back, and the engine kept rattling on at a slower rate. It coughed and died briefly several times, but Nelson kept the plane in the air and headed toward Karachi about 75 miles away. When Smith saw that the *New Orleans* was still airborne, he sped ahead to locate the destination landing place and circled so Nelson would not have to look for it. At last

Nelson saw the city ahead and landed before a large crowd. The plane was covered with oil from nose to tail, and there were a number of holes in the fabric.

When the world fliers arrived in Karachi, a message from General Patrick was waiting. Permission to carry a passenger had been denied. The adventure was over for Wells. But there was more bad news waiting for him. He was fired for disobeying his boss at Associated Press who had told him to relinquish the chase to another reporter after reaching Calcutta. The six fliers prepared to go on without him.

Linton Wells rode in the Boston *from Calcutta to Karachi.* PICTORIAL HISTORIES

The New Orleans *landed at Karachi, India (now Pakistan), with a broken engine connecting rod.* C.V. GLINES

The New Orleans *was drenched with oil from an exhaust valve dropping inside a piston causing it to break.* C.V. GLINES

Chapter 7
Calcutta to Vienna

The intense heat was extremely debilitating for the Cruiser crews in India. When they arrived at Karachi on July 4, they wanted to stay only long enough to install new engines before attempting the next leg over the forbidding mountains of Baluchistan and Persia (later Iran). They had landed at the airfield of a large British Royal Air Force repair depot and worked the next two days on their planes. On July 5 they were honored at a banquet sponsored by the RAF. No work was scheduled the next day, a Sunday, so they all slept in, hoping to make an early departure the next day.

The planes, now all reconditioned for the trip, left the ground at 6:30 a.m. and arrived at Chabar at 12:30.

Everything had gone so nicely that we hastily refueled, left at 2:30 and arrived at the small seaport town of Bandar Abbas (in Persia on the Gulf of Oman) at 6:30, Arnold reported in his diary. *The whole trip was over the same kind of country—absolutely barren of all vegetation excepting date trees and cactus. There were great stretches of sand, sand hills, ancient lava flows, some 5,000-foot mountains. The most lonesome, barren and desolate place imaginable.*

They stayed overnight at the home of the British consul and made a hasty get-away next morning at 5:30 a.m., destination: the seaport city of Bushire on the Persian Gulf. It was a

The Boston, *viewed from another airplane, somewhere over Asia.* C.V. GLINES VIA U.S. AIR FORCE

The cruisers flying along the shore of the Gulf of Oman on the way to Baghdad.
PICTORIAL HISTORIES

four-hour flight over a depressing, forbidding landscape. Jack Harding commented, "the country we passed over between Bandar Abbas and Bushire was the most vicious we had seen."

They were greeted by the American consul at Bushire who volunteered to send to town for sandwiches. Meanwhile, the planes were serviced, and since the sandwiches had not arrived and they were anxious to move on, took off for Baghdad, Mesopotamia (later Iraq), where the waters of the Tigris and Euphrates Rivers merge and flow into the gulf. Called "the cradle of civilization," the crews landed and found that Baghdad as seen in the movies or from the air is vastly different from Baghdad on the ground. The city that looked so magical and picturesque with its minarets and mosques from three thousand feet was really only a city of mud huts "full of British troops and town-bred Bedouins," according to Erik Nelson.

The group stayed at the large RAF base where "everyone was out to greet us, fed us cold drinks and sandwiches while we performed the routine work and then took us to their mess for dinner," Arnold noted in his diary for July 8. "Everyone was so tired and I remember getting into bed but don't remember lying down. Most of us are suffering from sunburned knees for at Karachi, we had adopted the English shorts."

The next stop was Aleppo, Syria, then a mandate of the French, and the three Cruisers took off at 11 a.m. They were escorted for the first hour and a half by a formation of five RAF planes. They followed the Euphrates River and saw scores of "sand devils" whirling across the desert below. The air was extremely turbulent, and one mountainous sand devil forced them up to six thousand feet. After six hours of flying, they landed at the French airdrome north of the city where they were greeted by French officers who insisted they drink some special wine they had saved for the occasion.

The fliers worked on their planes until dark and then were taken to a hotel in downtown Aleppo for the night. As had been their custom, they arose early and were off at 6 a.m. for the 600-mile flight across the mountainous terrain of Asia Minor to Constantinople (later Istanbul, Turkey). Down below were many miles of cultivated lands and then a desert where they saw many long camel caravans trudging along. Ahead was the snow-capped Taurus Mountain range that towered to 10,000 feet. Smith in the lead climbed to 4,000 feet and followed the Berlin-Baghdad Railroad through the passes which were so narrow that the pilots felt their wing tips were uncomfortably close to the sides. The temperature was near freezing, the first cold air they had felt since leaving the Kurile Islands. They landed at the airport, their first stop in Europe, where they were greeted by the American ambassador to Turkey Lt. Harry Halverson, the advance man for the Middle East portion of the flight, and Major Carlyle Wash, the advance officer for the European flight ahead. As usual, the men worked on their planes first and then were transported to a hotel in town for dinner. They planned originally to stay four days in Constantinople, but they were anxious to reach Paris by Bastille Day, a national holi-

The airport at Baghdad, Mesopotamia (now Iraq). PICTORIAL HISTORIES

French officials greeted the airmen at the Muslimi Aerodrome in Aleppo, Syria, on July 9. Syria was a French mandate at the time. MUSEUM OF FLYING

The fliers with dignitaries in Constantinople, Turkey, on July 24.
PICTORIAL HISTORIES

The Boston *flies through the Taurus Mountains on the way from Aleppo to Constantinople.*
PICTORIAL HISTORIES

day in France. Instead of leaving the next morning, July 11, the Turks asked that they stay another night, so they could inspect their planes. The airmen made a quick sightseeing trip in the morning and then spent more than an hour allowing the Turk officers to see the planes and answer their questions. They spent the evening quietly, writing letters and getting a much–needed rest. They had covered more than 15, 200 miles and had about 11,000 miles to go.

The three World Cruisers left Constantinople early on July 12 for Bucharest, Rumania. Ahead were the foothills of the Transylvanian Alps. They landed on the airdrome of the Franco–Romanian Aero Co. after about four hours of flying, but there was no one on hand to meet them. To their surprise, they had not been expected. Telegrams that Smith had sent from Aleppo and Constantinople had not been received. Smith telephoned the American consul who explained that he thought they were still many miles away in Southeast Asia. He hurried to the field while the fliers refueled the planes, much relieved that they didn't have a crowd pushing around them as they worked.

An impromptu dinner was held that night, and the chief of the Rumanian Air Service arrived to apologize on behalf of the government. "We found Bucharest to be a clean, snappy looking city, with sidewalk cafes just like Paris," Les Arnold said. "We were particularly impressed with the Rumanian Air Service and found that this tiny Balkan state had more airplanes ready for service than America!"

The six Americans were up at 3 a.m. on July 13 and off the ground by 6 a.m., headed for Vienna with a quick stop at Budapest, Hungary, for lunch. They headed west until they reached the Danube River and followed it to Belgrade on the plains of Serbia which had by then become Jugoslavia. They could have landed but had not arranged a stop there. They had plenty of fuel to continue, and the engines were humming perfectly, so they flew on to Budapest. As planned, they stopped only long enough for lunch and found there were only a few spectators on hand. They were told that a large crowd had been there to greet them in the morning, but a rumor was passed that the Americans were not coming until the next day so the people had dispersed. After paying their respects to Hungarian officials, the Americans were off for Vienna.

The arrival at Vienna's main airport was different from the others. A large crowd had gathered in front of the hangars. To the surprise of the fliers, the greeters were mostly American tourists, all equipped with cameras, insisting

Up the valley of the Danube River and across the plains of Hungary, on their way to Budapest. PICTORIAL HISTORIES

that the fliers pose with them individually and collectively. They were delayed getting any respite until dusk.

The airmen reached the city shortly after seven o'clock and were taken for a quick drive to see the sights and then to the Imperial Hotel, one of the most luxurious they had visited so far. "The size and furnishings of the room, the wonderful food, and the excellent service all made a great impression on us after some of the places we have recently stopped at," Arnold wrote in his diary. "Next morning four visitors and the six of us had breakfast in our private parlor. Although there were ten of us, we only took up a bit of one corner. They served us bowls of raspberries and cream, and it was almost worth flying around the world to eat them."

While they were in India, Smith had promised the others that if they could gain an extra day and arrive in Paris twenty–four hours ahead of their schedule, they could take a day's holiday in Paris. But instead of gaining one day, they had gained four and Paris was only a day's flight away. Arnold wrote, "So we left Vienna in high spirits."

U. S. FLIERS MAY REACH VIENNA THIS AFTERNOON

By The Associated Press.
Vienna, July 12.—The American round the world fliers are expected to reach Vienna tomorrow afternoon.

The United States army aviators, who reached Bucharest at 12:30 o'clock Saturday afternoon have Belgrade as their next stopping place, a distance of 290 miles from Bucharest, then Budapest, 220 miles, and Vienna, 140—a total of 650 miles.

A large crowd inspects the DWCs at the Vienna, Austria, main airport. C.V. GLINES

Chapter 8
On to Paris, London and the North Atlantic

It was an early take off again on the morning of July 14 under a dark overcast sky. The destination was Strasbourg, a French city that had been regained from the Germans after the Armistice. After about ten minutes of flight the three planes ran into heavy rain and flew through dark skies all the way across Austria and Germany.

Occasionally we dived through banks of fog that lasted for ten or fifteen minutes, Wade said. *The rain and fog drove us down to the river, and often we shot around sharp bends and kicked rudder just in time to avoid crashing unannounced into a castle. For several hours we followed the winding course of the Danube, flying against a stiff head wind that held us down to fifty miles an hour. When we were above the Black Forest, we suddenly shot out of the fog and gloom, and there in front of us, glistening like quicksilver, lay a river famous in history and song. It was the Rhine, one of the great rivers of the world.*

The planes stayed in Strasbourg only long enough to take on gas and oil. The fliers took off without visiting the city and flew over Nancy, then swung north over the quiet battlefields of the "war to end all wars." They saw the trenches, fortifications and shell holes at Verdun, Argonne, Rheims and St. Mihiel.

They turned north from Nancy along the Hindenburg Line and were nearing Paris when a flight of French planes intercepted them and escorted them to the famous City of Light. As a gesture of respect, the Americans circled over the Arc de Triomphe and landed at Le Bourget Airport at 5:30 p.m. where more than 5,000 cheering, flag-waving Frenchmen were waiting for them. It was July 14, Bastille Day, and the crowd was in a festive mood. First to reach them was Major Carlyle Wash, American military attaché.

An hour passed before we could get a chance to do any work on our planes, Wade said, *because it took that long for us to shake hands with the many high officials and foreign diplomats who had come out to greet us. During that hour on the outskirts of Paris we met more generals, ambassadors, cabinet ministers, and celebrities than we had encountered in all the rest of our lives.*

Flying time for that day was ten hours 25 minutes. They had reached Paris in 12 days flying from Calcutta, a distance of 6,163 miles. After the planes were refueled, the weary airmen were whisked to their hotel where they hurriedly washed up, had a quick dinner and then were ushered into a box at the Folies Bergeres. Dead tired after such a long day, they settled in their seats comfortably and promptly fell asleep. Awakened when the show was over, they returned to the hotel and printed a sign that was placed on each room door:

PLEASE DO NOT WAKE US UNTIL NINE O'CLOCK TOMORROW MORNING UNLESS THIS HOTEL IS ON FIRE AND NOT EVEN THEN UNLESS THE FIREMEN HAVE GIVEN UP ALL HOPE.

Although the six Americans had hoped to rest and see the sights, they received no relief from the duties that protocol demanded. Wade explained:

At ten o'clock we went to the Arc de Triomphe and placed a wreath on the tomb of the French Unknown Soldier. Then we started on a round of official calls, visited the President of France, attended a private luncheon and various ceremonies, went to two teas, and finally banqueted until midnight.

Nevertheless, we did enjoy our day in Paris thoroughly, Wade added. *For instance, what*

Lt. Ogden unveils the French Tricolor flag after the Boston *landed at Le Bourget Aerodrome in Paris.*
PETER M. BOWERS COLLECTION

A huge crowd awaited the world fliers at Paris, Le Bourget Aerodrome.
PETER M. BOWERS COLLECTION

U.S. 'ROUND-THE-WORLD FLIERS SAFE IN PARIS

By The Associated Press

Paris, July 14.—The United States army fliers who are circling the globe swept over Paris this afternoon and landed safely at Le Bourget airdome, 19 days behind schedule, but with a gain of 12 days to their credit since they left Tokio.

They will not remain here long, but will proceed to London, and from there, flying by way of Orkney island and Greenland Labrador and Quebec, will go speeding back to the homeland.

Wade and Smith with officials at Paris. PETER M. BOWERS COLLECTION VIA U.S. AIR FORCE

Lt. Ogden with a tin of Mobiloil finishes servicing his plane at Paris.

Lt. Wade conferring with French officials upon his arrival in Paris.

Two of the airmen, wearing the short pants they had picked up in India, are greeted upon their arrival in Paris. Ogden is on the left, Nelson on the right. Below, Gen. John J. Pershing entertains the fliers on July 15 at the famous Paris restaurant Foyot's. PETER M. BOWERS COLLECTION VIA U.S. AIR FORCE

*could have been more delightful for six lieu-
tenants than the luncheon at which we were
the guests of General Pershing? He put his
arms around us, told us funny stories and
proved himself a genial host and a regular
fellow!*

They also met France's President Domergue, expecting to stay only a few minutes. However, they stayed an hour, and then the president invited them to meet the athletes at the Olympic Games being held near Paris. Afterwards, he wanted to present them each with the Legion of Honor, but Smith explained that they could not accept foreign decorations without the special consent of Congress. Instead, the president gave them each an autographed photograph of himself. That night they attended a banquet at the Allied Club and afterward went to Maxim's and Montmartre "for old times' sake," Arnold scribbled in his diary for July 15.

Next morning, the fliers were at Le Bourget to find the field had been decorated in their honor, and a number of French and American diplomatic officials were there to see them off. They left for London at exactly 11 a.m. Two airliners loaded with passengers took off at the same time, and a flight of French fighter planes joined up, so there were a dozen planes flying in loose formation until the fighters withdrew near the French coast. The three Cruisers continued with the airliners, occasionally waving at the passengers sitting comfortably in their enclosed cabins.

They climbed to 7,000 feet where it was uncomfortably cold for the world fliers in their open cockpits, a reminder of what was ahead of them over the Atlantic. When they landed at Croydon Airport after the 215–mile flight, the fliers found that the passengers on the airliners were mostly American tourists.

The landing was made shortly after 2 p.m., and the fliers were besieged by photographers, reporters and autograph hunters. On hand were the American attache, RAF representatives and British officials. A hundred London "bobbies" joined hands and formed a ring around the men and escorted them to the dining facility. Afterwards, they refueled their planes and were driven to the RAF Club in London. That evening they were the guests of honor at a Royal Air Force dinner.

The three DWCs just before takeoff from Paris on July 16. The next stop would be London.
PETER M. BOWERS COLLECTION VIA U.S. AIR FORCE

BRITISH AVIATOR IN WORLD FLIGHT MISSING AT SEA

Japanese Destroyers Search in Vain for Any Trace of MacLaren; London Government Thinks Him Safe.

U. S. AIRMEN AT LONDON

Two-Thirds of Their 'Round-World Flight Completed; Will Spend Week in Preparation for Next Stretch.

By The Associated Press.

Tokio, July 17.—Japanese destroyers have not yet found any trace of A. Stuart MacLaren, the British aviator, and his companion, who left Yetorofu Island early yesterday morning for Paramashiru Island, Kuriles, a flight of 450 miles. British officials, however, do not believe the aviators are in any danger.

It is thought possible that they may have landed at Broughton bay, Shimushiru Island, one of the smaller of the Kurile group, about half way between Yetorofu and Paramashiru. Lieutenant Colonel L. G. Broome, who blazed the trail for MacLaren and who accompanied him on his present flight, laid a supply base at Broughton bay in case of necessity.

Americans at London.

London, July 16.—Six bronzed American bird men, 244 flying hours out of Seattle and with two-thirds of the world's circumference behind them, glided into the Croyden airdrome just outside of London this afternoon, ready for their first real rest on the round-the-globe flight and for a week of preparation for their final dash across the Atlantic via Iceland and Greenland.

They left the Lebourget airdrome outside Paris at 11.05 o'clock this morning, fought head winds all the way across the English channel but jumped from the continent in otherwise perfect flying condition and landed at the British airdrome just three hours and four minutes later to be greeted by a crowd of enthusiasts who nearly mobbed them as they climbed stiffly from their cockpits.

Will Get New Engines.

Tomorrow the planes will go to Brough for the installation of new engines and for a general tightening up process before they hop off some time next week for Kirkwall, in the Orkneys, the last European stop.

The aviators' arrival was most casual, their only escort being a British passenger plane and several French military planes.

The aviators, tanned by the sun, looked to be the better off for their 18,000-mile flight.

"It's an experience I wouldn't take a million for, but I wouldn't start over again for a million,"—Lieutenant Arnold said.

The world fliers on their way to London from Paris.
PETER M. BOWERS COLLECTION VIA U.S. AIR FORCE

One of the DWCs in the foreground, escorted by a British aircraft arriving at London. C.V. GLINES

The DWCs parked at Croydon Aerodrome at London, July 25. U.S. AIR FORCE MUSEUM

The fliers were back at Croydon and left for Brough near the seaport of Hull next morning at 11:15, a 165–mile flight. It was one of the most pleasant trips they had made as they sped across the landscape over industrial areas and green fields. A number of pilots in small planes came up to fly formation briefly, wave and then depart. The landing at Brough was on a small test field used by the Blackbrun Aircraft Corporation which was well equipped with machine shops, equipment, and comfortable quarters. The fliers were met by a small but enthusiastic gathering of local townspeople and airport workers.

While they had been in Constantinople, the fliers received the first information about the assistance that would be provided by the U.S. Navy across the Atlantic. The escort ships would not be in place until July 28, which meant a delay of eleven days after they landed at Brough. The engines on all three aircraft were removed and replaced by new ones on the day of arrival, and pontoons again replaced the wheels.

There was now time for rest and relaxation, but there were many invitations that they were expected to accept. A great banquet was to be held at the Savoy Hotel the next day, sponsored by the Royal Aero Club. "We were about as well-equipped with clothes as the head hunters of Borneo," Arnold said. "Smith ordered me to sprint up to London and assemble a few spare parts for our wardrobe."

Smith and Wade joined Arnold that day, while Nelson, Harding and Ogden elected to work on the planes and visit London later in the week. The banquet that night "was a regular high-hat spiel-fest, with Lords and Earls and Dukes accompanied by their ladies, Arnold reported.

Working on a DWC at Brough on the Humber, where pontoons replaced the wheels and major overhauls were conducted on the three aircraft at facilities of the Blackburn Aeroplane Company.
MUSEUM OF FLYING

The airmen were guests of the Tharratt family at Brough during their stay there.
MUSEUM OF FLYING

To their surprise and delight, the Prince of Wales happened to be having dinner upstairs and sent word he would like to meet them. They were escorted to his suite and had an amiable chat with him. He said he expected to visit America shortly and hoped to be on Long Island to greet them. After the banquet, they were taken on a night trip around London by American newspaper correspondents, caught a train back to Brough next morning and got back to work on their planes.

On July 22, there was an accident that almost had a fatal result. Smith explains:

We were taking off the landing gear and putting pontoons on the Chicago and in order to do this we used a crane and a heavy chain to lift her up on the dolly. As we had to get right in under the plane to do some work while it hung suspended in the air, we first tested the chain. It stood a strain of six and a half tons, and as the plane only weighed two and a half, we naturally thought it more than strong enough.

We had to work in a cramped position, so several of us took turns. A moment after we

had crawled out, the chain broke, and the plane crashed to the floor. Why it took a notion to break at that particular moment, we don't know. Of course, it was nobody's fault. It was just one of those things that occur without one's being able to prevent them. The pontoons were badly damaged, so we had to take them off and put on new ones. Fortunately, there was another set, the ones that had been sent from America for Major Martin's Seattle.

U. S. FLYERS RESUME THEIR JOURNEY TODAY

By The Associated Press.
Kirkwall, Orkney Islands, July 29.—Everything is in readiness to take care of the world flyers when they arrive here tomorrow. Stores of oil, gasoline and stocked rafts are awaiting the airplanes. Tow-boats and repair men are being kept at Houton Bay landing stage in the event they are needed. Arrangements have been made so that the flyers can leave in 18 hours if necessary.

News that the airmen are certain to arrive Wednesday relieved the tension in this outlying town, undergone because of continual delays in the aviators' plans for hopping off from Brough.

The day before takeoff from Kirkwall in the Orkney Islands the airmen visited the scuttled World War One German warships at Scapa Flow. Here Wade falls into the water while attempting to leap from one gun to another on the German flagship. Arnold and Harding are watching from the other gun barrel.
U.S. AIR FORCE MUSEUM

The group worked each day but took time to tour the area, shop and enjoy the good food. They purchased heavy flying clothes and cleaned up odds and ends on the planes. On the 23rd, they were invited to a garden party by the King and Queen at Buckingham Palace in London but declined respectfully because they were concerned about the weather that lay ahead and decided to await word from Admiral Thomas F. Magruder, commander of the escort ships, about the arrangements for the flight to Iceland. But the word did not come that day, nor for the next week. Finally, on the evening of the 29th, they were told to expect to leave next morning.

The planes were given a short test hop and tied up at their moorings in the Humber River for refueling. At 10:30, the three planes with Smith leading took off into the fog and mist out over the North Sea that dissipated in about an hour. They flew over many beach resorts, beautiful estates and crumbling ru-

ins en route to the Orkney Islands, an archipelago of about 70 islands in the Atlantic ocean and the North Sea. They landed at a small harbor off Scapa Flow near Kirkwall where they were met by the *U.S.S. Richmond*, flagship for Admiral Magruder and his fleet of escort ships. The *Richmond* had prepared moorings according to prior instructions, and the details of the Navy's cooperation were carefully discussed with the fliers. They planned to leave the following day, July 30, for Hornafjord, Iceland, but the fog was too dense. August 1 was a repeat of the day before with fog reported along the route thus preventing any thought of flying the 555 miles to Hornafjord. They all knew that the weather across the North Atlantic would be more hazardous than the trip down the Aleutians.

The USS Richmond, *the main escort ship used in the North Atlantic.* C.V. GLINES

AMERICAN FLYERS OFF FOR ICELAND

Start From Kirkwall Made at 6:18 This Morning; Ready for Arrival.

By The Associated Press.
Kirkwall, Orkney Islands, Scotland, Aug. 2.—The United States world flyers left here today for Iceland. They took off from Houton bay for the 500-mile trip at 6:18 a. m.

Arnold, Smith and Wade relax aboard the USS Richmond *at Scapa Flow before their dangerous trip across the North Atlantic.* U.S. AIR FORCE MUSEUM

Just before the DWCs takeoff for Iceland on August 2, citizens of the Orkney Islands came down to the dock to see them off. U.S. AIR FORCE MUSEUM

Chapter 9
The Loss of the
Boston

The weather was better at Kirkwall on August 2 but marginal farther west. Smith decided they would go, and the three planes began their takeoffs. The official report of the flight tells what happened next:

The Chicago *in attempting to take off, had considerable difficulty in getting up on the step of the pontoons and could not do so until the* Boston *came down, landing directly in front. This created sufficient roughness of water and currents of air to help the* Chicago *off. The flight started at 8:34 a.m.*

Fog was encountered within five miles after departure, and finding it impossible to go under, the flight climbed above the fog, continuing on the course for about 30 minutes when all three planes were trapped in a heavy fog. It was impossible for the planes to see each other. The Chicago *and* Boston, *using their instruments, climbed and turned back out of the fog, coming out at an altitude of 2,800 feet, where they circled for about 30 minutes looking for the* New Orleans. *Fearing some accident had befallen Nelson and Harding, the two returned to Kirkwall, dropping a note at the hotel to immediately give out information regarding the separation.*

Smith and Wade landed at Kirkwall to wait to see if the *Richmond* had any information about the missing plane. Fearing the worst, everyone was relieved when a radio message was received from Nelson that he was safe and sound at Hornafjord. The message said:

GOT INTO PROPELLER WASH AND NEAR TAIL SPIN CAME OUT JUST ABOVE WATER PAST FOG BELT ARRIVED FIVE THIRTY SEVEN   NELSON

Nelson had had a very close call. When the other planes failed to appear, he had forged ahead on a compass course over a fog bank for more than three hours. The fog ended abruptly, the sky became clear and Nelson and Harding sighted a U.S. destroyer. Harding wrote a note asking if there was any news about Smith and Wade and requested they verify by signals that they were headed in the right direction. He put the message into a bag and aimed at the ship's deck but it fell into the sea. He wrote a second one and it landed on the deck. A few minutes later, they got hand signals that no other planes had passed in that direction. They passed the cruiser *Raleigh* and flew above another fog belt that hid the sea for the rest of the way to Iceland. The weather cleared again as they neared the coast and saw the village of Hornafjord dead ahead. They landed, moored the plane at prepositioned buoys and hurried ashore by boat to await the *Chicago* and *Boston*. There they found some of the sailors from the *U.S.S. Raleigh* who had been left there to set up a temporary radio station which was also to be used as the fliers' quarters.

The *Chicago* and *Boston* left next morning under clear skies and a welcome tail wind. At a point between the Faeroe and Orkney Islands, the *Boston* was to the right and slightly behind the *Chicago* cruising along easily when Wade saw the needle on the oil pressure gauge slowing retreating to zero. He knew they were in for a forced landing. He turned the plane into the wind and glided to a smooth landing on the ocean. Smith circled, and when he saw that Wade had brought the plane in safely on top of a huge swell, he flew low overhead to see what signals Wade would give. He saw oil on the water and all over the plane and knew what had happened.

Leigh signaled frantically for us not to land, Arnold said. *Because of the swell he figured that if we came down beside him we would never get off again, and then we would both*

ANOTHER CASUALTY SUFFERED BY UNITED STATES AIR FLEET IN ITS AROUND-WORLD FLIGHT

Plane of Lieutenant Wade Is Forced Down Half Way Between Kirkwall and Iceland Coast; Is Wrecked.

COMMANDER SMITH SAFE

Successfully Negotiates 500 Miles to Hornafjord and Rejoins Lieutenant Nelson Who Made Trip Saturday.

On Board U. S. S. Richmond, Aug. 3.—By Wireless to the Associated Press.—The machine of Lieutenant Wade was wrecked by an accident while the cruiser Richmond was trying to salvage it.

The plane probably cannot be used again.

The wings of the machine were severely damaged in alighting. The plane drifted about in the rough windy seas for four hours. It was picked up by a British trawler and taken in tow to the torpedo boat destroyer Billingsley and finally reached the Richmond.

The cruiser, in trying to hoist the plane, badly damaged it. A portion of the lifting apparatus broke, sending down a steel boom weighing a ton, which broke the propeller and pierced a pontoon.

Two haggard and weary men, Lieutenant Wade and Sergeant Ogden, stood on the deck of the Richmond and saw their hopes of completing the flight finally vanish after a nineteen thousand mile journey around the globe.

Abandon Hope Reluctantly.

Hope for saving the plane was not abandoned immediately, although conditions rendered its salvage almost impossible, the rising sea forcing the plane against the cruisers' side. Efforts were made to save all things movable on board, but as the storm heightened captain Cotton of the Richmond des in his salvage attempt and

plane against the cruisers' side. Efforts were made to save all things movable on board, but as the storm heightened captain Cotton of the Richmond des in his salvage attempt and told Lieutenant Wade it he believed it worth while he would moor the plane at the end of a long line and have the cruiser lay to until morning.

Later it was decided to pierce the pontoons and sink the plane, but the evident distress of Lieutenant Wade and Sergeant Ogden caused a change in this plan and the captain ordered the machine towed to the Sudero Island.

Both Lieutenant Wade and Sergeant Ogden strove desperately to make repairs to their craft while floating 70 miles from the nearest port, cold and battered by the waves. They had no thought of quitting the flight until the accident to the plane alongside the Richmond, although the structure of the plane had been weakened by the two hours of towing. Both men were in the plane six hours, after alighting on the water, working hard to make the craft right to take the air again.

Smith Reaches Iceland.

By The Associated Press.

Hornafjord, Iceland, Aug. 3.—The second American world flier, Lieutenant Lowell H. Smith, arrived here from Kirkwall, Orkney Islands, at 10:37 p. m. today. The third plane, piloted by Lieutenant Leigh Wade, failed to complete the flight when he was forced down into the water about midway between Iceland and the Orkneys.

Wade came down approximately midway between the Orkneys and Iceland. A trawler found and took his plane in tow.

Weather Favorable for Start.

By The Associated Press.

Kirkwall, Scotland, Aug. 3.—Under perfect weather conditions in the Orkney Islands, Lieutenants Lowell Smith and Leigh Wade left the Scapa Flow at 9:17 o'clock this morning on their second attempt to reach Hoefn Hornafjord, Iceland, where Lieutenant Nelson made a jump yesterday through the fog, while Smith and Wade had to return here.

Smith and his mechanic, Sergeant Ogden, had difficulty in rising from the water.

When the airmen finally got up they were saluted by the whistle of the

The USS Billingsley *is shown towing the downed* Boston. *The plane was soon turned over to the cruiser* USS Richmond. MUSEUM OF FLIGHT

be helpless in the middle of the ocean. But we did hate to leave them sitting out there in that remote part of the North Atlantic. However, after circling round once or twice we headed off on our course and flew with the throttle wide open to the nearest destroyer, which was over a hundred miles away, near the Faeroe Islands.

As we passed over the Faeroes we saw a telegraph line, which we followed around Sydero Island until we came to a village where we dropped a message. A bit north of the Faeroes we picked up the Billingsley. *But before we reached her, Lowell had written two notes, each identical, describing Wade's mishap, the peril he and Ogden were in, their approximate location, time of landing, and the condition of both sea and wind, so that the naval officers could estimate how far the wind might blow them in the interval before a rescue could be effected.*

The first note we put in a message bag and dropped on the Billingsley, *but she was making fully twenty knots and I missed her deck by several yards. We had only one note left,*

and every moment was precious. It was imperative that this one should get to the destroyer, so I tied it to my one and only life preserver. When I dropped it this time, I again missed the deck, but a sailor dived overboard and fished it out of the sea.

The note ended with a request that if they understood our message and were ready to start at once to the rescue, they were to give us three blasts from the whistle. We circled around, saw the captain seize the message, read it, and run across the deck. A moment later we saw three long streaks of steam coming from the whistle, and almost at the same moment clouds of smoke poured from the funnels, and the destroyer shot ahead like a greyhound whose leash had been slipped.

As the *Billingsley* raced ahead at 31 knots, the captain radioed the *Richmond* which immediately started to the rescue area. Smith and Arnold had done all they could. They turned on course for Hornafjord flying through rain with very poor visibility over the entire 250 miles. They passed the destroyer *Reid*, positioned halfway between the Faeroes and Iceland without seeing it. Smith located the harbor at Horn-afjord and landed hurriedly, anxious to hear if the rescue ships had found Wade and Ogden.

Meanwhile, the *Boston* was wallowing help-lessly in the heavy swells. Wade describes what happened when they landed:

When we reached the water, I discovered how deceitful the sea is when you are above it. At five hundred feet it had looked fairly smooth. But when we landed, we found it so rough that the left pontoon nearly wrapped itself around the lower wing, and snapped two of the vertical wires.

At first I though the oil tank had burst and let the entire supply drop out. But it was still full. So we knew that our trouble was due to the failure of the oil pump. This meant that our repairs could not be made at sea.

Smith and Les were circling around us, and I was afraid that they might land and crack up also. That was why we signaled so em-phatically for them to stay in the air. We in-dicated to them that our engine had failed, that our repairs could not be made at sea, and that they should go on.

The first thing we did, after they had left, was to fasten the anchor to the bridle and heave it overboard. We hadn't been bobbing up and down on the waves for many minutes before we discovered what a nasty business it is to be in mid–ocean on a fragile plane with the waves hitting her at right angles. Soon we both grew dizzy. But we realized that unless the vertical wires were repaired, the ship might not ride out the sea until help arrived. So we managed to crawl onto the wing and get them fixed. Then, climbing back into our cockpits, we settled down for a little rest.

Wade and Ogden had landed just before 11 a.m. and, knowing the approximate positions of the *Richmond* and *Billingsley*, thought it would be late afternoon before they would be located. In mid–afternoon, Wade saw a whisp of smoke on the horizon. They both crawled on the top wing, and Wade signaled with a piece of canvas while Ogden fired off several flares from a Very pistol. The smoke gradually disappeared below the horizon.

They both were confident they would soon be rescued but gradually began to realize that they were mere specks on the vast ocean and wondered what their fate was to be. "Never in our lives had either of us felt so lonesome, so helpless," Wade reported later.

As they wondered what to do, the sea be-came choppy, and it looked as though the wings would dip down into the waves and buckle un-der the weight. Hour after hour they waited, and Wade saw another whisp of smoke on the horizon. Ogden yanked a piece of wood from the rear of the fuselage, attached a piece of cloth to it and started wigwagging furiously. Wade fired some flares. The ship slowly turned to-ward them. It was a British fishing trawler, the *Rugby–Ramsey*, that gradually came alongside.

They had been fortunate. They had landed near a course taken by fishing boats plying be-tween the Orkneys and Faeroes, and the trawler attempted to tow them toward them. But each time the trawler went up on a wave, she seemed to stand still and the *Boston* would swing around and head into the wind. When the trawler would drop from the crest of the swell, the *Boston* would be jerked violently. The pontoons would disappear under the water.

After a half hour of this, the trawler found that she wasn't making any headway, so they stopped towing and simply stood by await-ing the arrival of one of our destroyers, Wade explained. *In a little while the* Billingsley *arrived and we cast adrift from the* Rugby-Ramsey *in order to pick up the destroyer's line. Then a few minutes later the* Richmond *raced up. Again we switched over, and in transferring to the Admiral's cruiser one of our wings dipped under a wave and the ribs of the trailing edge popped like the crackle of a machine gun.*

As they pulled alongside the *Richmond*, a crane with a sling attached was dropped down, and Ogden attached it to the plane's lifting hook. Wade and Ogden climbed aboard the ship, con-fident that they would be taken back to Kirkwall, have the *Boston* repaired and then chase after the *Chicago* and *New Orleans*.

While they watched, there was a sudden crashing noise. The tackle on the crane broke loose from the main mast ,and the plane fell back

The Boston *is shown about to be hoisted aboard the* USS Richmond. *The aircraft was raised about four feet out of the water when the boom broke, breaking the propeller and putting a hole in a pontoon. The damage was too great, however, and after a tow by the* Richmond *to within a mile of land, the* Boston *sank.* C.V. GLINES

The Boston *just before sinking into the North Atlantic.* C.V. GLINES

into the water. The pontoons cracked from the impact. Several sailors tried to make emergency patches on the wood veneer while others operated a bilge pump. Wade and Ogden took everything loose off the plane and decided to try to disassemble it by detaching the wings and pontoons before trying again to hoist the fuselage onto the deck.

As they all worked furiously, the wind increased, and the plane was thrown about in the angry sea. One sailor was washed off the pontoons, but two of his shipmates quickly seized him before he drifted away. Everyone was hauled aboard, and it was decided to try to tow the plane to one of the Faeroe Islands and repair it there. As the tow started, Wade and Ogden watched it thrashing up and down until midnight. Then, exhausted, they went below to sleep. About five o'clock in the morning they were awakened and told that the plane had capsized. The spreader bar that held the pontoons apart had broken allowing them to smash together. Fearing that this might happen, Wade and Ogden had left all the tanks open so they would fill with water and cause the plane to sink instead of drifting and become a menace to shipping.

When this occurred we were within a mile of land, Wade said. *So near and yet so far! Alas, we were forced to abandon her, and at 5:30 a.m. we cut the towlines, bade farewell to our friend who had carried us so far round the globe, and headed for Iceland with heavy hearts.*

The bad news was radioed to Smith and Nelson at Hornafjord.

We were all torn between two emotions, one of relief that Wade and Ogden were safe, Arnold wrote in his diary. *And the other of sorrow that after coming 20,000 miles they should so suddenly lose their plane through absolutely no fault of theirs.*

TWO PLANES TO CONTINUE WORLD FLIGHT TOGETHER

No Prospect That Wrecked Ship Will Be Repaired.

By the Associated Press.

Hoefn Hornafjord, Iceland, Aug. 4.—Lieutenant Lowell H. Smith and Lieutenant Erick Nelson, the United States army's globe fliers, are ready if the present favorable weather conditions continue, to jump off within the next 24 hours for their 300 mile jaunt around the southern coast of Iceland and thence northward to the harbor of Reykjavik. The two planes were given a thorough examination today and found to be in prime condition.

Lieutenants Smith and Nelson expressed regret over the mishap to their comrade flier, Lieutenant Leigh Wade, who was forced down Sunday by engine trouble as he was endeavoring to negotiate the route across the North Atlantic from Scotland, and whose plane was wrecked in an attempt to hoist it on board the cruiser Richmond.

During the day messages were received here from Wade, which indicated the possibility that his plane might be repaired so that he could continue his flight. Later in the afternoon, however, advices received from the Richmond indicated that the plane was so badly damaged that it was unlikely that it could be repaired.

MacLaren Continues by Boat.

Cordova, Alaska, Aug. 4.—Major A. Stuart MacLaren, British around the-world flyer, and his companions were en route tonight aboard the Canadian trawler Thiepval for Dutch Harbor, Amaknak Island, in the Aleutian group, after their plane was damaged beyond repair in a forced landing in fog near Nikolski, Komandorski Islands, Siberia, Saturday.

Chapter 10
The Most
Dangerous Legs

The news about the *Boston* saddened everyone connected with the world flight. The remaining four fliers knew how much Wade and Ogden had wanted to complete their mission and realized that their misfortune could have happened to them. There was nothing to do but tend to their own planes and continue. They were given accommodations in a fisherman's cottage where blankets and canned food had been accumulated by the advance officer. The sailors from the *Raleigh*, anchored 25 miles off-shore, prepared the meals, took care of their supplies and handled their radio messages.

The four fliers spent August 4 working on their planes and left the next morning for Reykjavik. They followed the coast and encountered a strong wind from the north which caused them to take five hours to fly the 290 miles. The flight was uneventful and the fliers landed among hundreds of small boats where buoys had been placed for mooring. An enthusiastic crowd and the Prime Minister of Iceland was waiting to greet them. A few minutes after they tied up, the *Richmond* steamed into the harbor with Wade and Ogden on board.

In addition to the *Richmond*, there were four other American warships in the Reykjavik harbor with about 2,500 sailors, the first time any American warships had ever visited there. The streets were crowded and there were many newspaper reporters following the fliers around. They found that the city was very modern with banks, good hotels, cafes, clubs, motion picture houses, taxis, shops and well-paved streets. The inhabitants were of Scandinavian descent, well-dressed and most could speak English with a pleasant accent.

On the evening of August 7, the group was invited to a buffet and dance aboard the *Richmond*. The next day they shopped for souvenirs, attended a luncheon given by the Prime Minister for Admiral Magruder and his staff. Meanwhile, they were waiting for reports from Lt. LeClair D. Schulze about arrangements at Angmagsalik, Greenland. He was on board the *Gertrud Rask*, a Danish steamer, but it was blocked in the ice and unable to reach its destination. It could be several days before the ice would break up so the cruiser *Raleigh* scouted along the route to see if there were any other harbors suitable for refueling the planes. Meanwhile, the fliers worked on their planes at Reykjavik and scanned the weather reports.

Radio messages were sent to Schulze who reported on August 14 that a safe mooring place had opened up at Angmagsalik but a few hours later had closed. On August 16, plans were made for the fliers to proceed to Fredricksdal, Greenland where an emergency base had been established. It would be a risky 835-mile flight, far off the shipping lanes and on the edge of the

World flight supply ship Hans Egedi at Minonak, Greenland. MUSEUM OF FLYING

Sailors from the Richmond *getting ready to bring the* New Orleans *up onto the beach for repairs at Reykjavik, Iceland.* C.V. GLINES

Hauling the New Orleans *through the streets of Reykjavik by truck.* C.V. GLINES

The airmen were greeted warmly by the citizens of Iceland. U.S. AIR FORCE MUSEUM

U. S. FLYERS COMPLETE ANOTHER LEG OF TRIP

By The Associated Press,
Reykjavik, Iceland, Aug. 5.—Skirting the southeastern, southern and southwestern coasts of Iceland, Lieutenant Lowell H. Smith and Lieutenant Erik Nelson today drove their 'round-the-world planes from Hoefn Hornafjord to Reykjavik, a distance of some 300 miles, in 4 hours and 58 minutes. The take-off from Hoefn Hornafjord to Reykjavik was made under good weather conditions and these continued throughout the journey, except for a heavy head wind encountered by the planes as they returned northward from the southern point of Iceland. The winds buffeted the fliers considerably, but nevertheless they were able to make a splendid landing at the spot assigned to them in the bay here.

Arctic where fogs and gales prevailed. Admiral Magruder ordered five American destroyers to patrol along the route spaced about 125 miles apart.

Their plans to take off from the water were delayed when Smith's plane broke a spreader bar between the pontoons and Nelson's propeller was split. All supplies and spares had been put on board the *Richmond* which had already put to sea to go to its assigned position so it had to return so repairs could be made.

That same day, the Italian aviator Lt. Antonio Locatelli and a crew of three arrived in a *Dornier Wal* airplane, intent upon flying around the world in the opposite direction. Locatelli had made no advance arrangements for his flight across the Atlantic and was relying upon supplies left over by the Americans. According to an agreement between officials in Washington and Italy, the Italian plane was to remain one flight behind the American planes. However, Locatelli asked if he would be allowed to accompany the Americans. Smith requested permission from General Patrick in Washington and it was granted.

The village of Angmagsalik on Greenland's east coast was supposed to be the fliers' next stop from Iceland, but the weather closed in this area. They had to fly on to Fredricksdal at the southern tip of the large island.
U.S. AIR FORCE MUSEUM

The Chicago *and the* New Orleans *moored in the iceberg-infested harbor at Fredricksdal, Greenland.* PICTORIAL HISTORIES

Locatelli's ill-fated monoplane.
PICTORIAL HISTORIES

On August 21, weather reports were at last favorable and the two Cruisers took off at 6:55 a.m., followed by the Italian plane. The *Dornier*, faster than the Cruisers, tried to stay in loose formation with them but had to circle occasionally until, apparently, Locatelli got impatient and sped ahead. He soon was out of sight and the Americans never saw the plane again.

The two American planes stayed on course and passed the *Richmond*, 90 miles out, then the *Reid*, 115 miles farther; the *Billingsley* 140 miles farther, and the *Barry* at 150 miles. When they passed the *Barry*, it was displaying a signal that there was dangerous weather ahead and the two planes quickly found out what that meant. They ran into a thick fog about 150 miles from the Greenland coast.

The account of this leg by Lowell Smith states:

We were forced to fly close to the water on account of the fog . But even then it was so thick that we flashed over the Raleigh. *without seeing her. Seventy-five miles out from Greenland we struck the first floes. As we neared the coast, the ice increased until we were flying over a seemingly endless expanse of fantastic bergs of every size and shape. Had we seen them under different conditions the sight, no doubt, would have inspired us. As it was, they were terrifying, because we never saw them until we were right upon them. . . .*

NEW BASE IN GREENLAND WATERS FOUND FOR U. S. WORLD FLYERS

Harbor Free From Ice Is Located South of Inaccessible Angmagsalik.

By The Associated Press.
Washington, Aug. 7.—An early resumption of the world flight by the two remaining planes, now at Reykjavik, Iceland, was expected in military circles today, following official information that the army advance party had located a safe substitute base for ice-locked Angmagsalik, which had been listed as the next terminal.

A dispatch from the cruiser Milwaukee relayed a report from the explorers declaring a satisfactory place

had been found at Ekaluit on the west coast of Greenland. Not only would this afford a secure landing place for the planes, the report said, but an open harbor was available for the Milwaukee and the facilities for hauling out the planes should moderate repairs be necessary.

The place did not appear even on maps of the general staff and considerable search was necessary before army officers finally identified it as the old post listed on Danish charts as "Hullek."

It is considerably farther south than the proposed base which the army advance was unable to reach because of unprecedented ice fields. Ekaluit was said to enjoy longer periods of open water and has been so recorded in marine journals.

The last stop in Greenland before flyng to North America was Ivigtut on the island's west shore. It was 335 miles to Icy Tickle on Labrador's shore. The Cruiser USS Milwaukee *is seen below the aircraft.*

PICTORIAL HISTORIES

Three times we came so suddenly upon huge icebergs that there was no time left to do any deciding. We simply jerked the wheel back for a quick climb, and we were lucky enough to zoom over the top of it into the still denser fog above. Here we were completely lost and unable to see beyond the prop and wing tips. Blindly we would grope and feel our way downward, hoping against hope that the little space we should eventually descend into just above the surface of the water would be clear of ice for a great enough distance to enable us to glance around, size up the situation, and get set for dodging the next one. . . .

But finally what we feared would happen did happen. Diving through a small patch of extra heavy fog that was clinging close to the water, we emerged on the other side to find ourselves plunging straight toward a wall of white. The New Orleans *was close behind us with that huge berg looming in front. I banked steeply to the right while Erik and Jack swung sharply to the left. Both left wings seemed to graze the edge of the berg as we shot past it. And in far less time than it takes to tell it the two planes were lost from each other.*

Smith stayed on course, while Nelson swung left out to sea before resuming his course to Fredricksdal. For the next hour, the two, on their own, dodged icebergs and then the white shadows occasionally changed to black which meant they had reached land. Several times, while steering clear of the dark shadows which were cliffs along the shoreline, they would turn and find a white shadow sliding by on their left. It would be a berg that they had missed by only a few feet. They broke out into the clear briefly and then had to climb above a dense fog that was down to the water level and couldn't be flown under. As they arrived near where they thought Fredricksdal should be, a hole in the clouds opened up and both planes landed beside the *Island Falk*, a Danish coast guard cutter that would be used as a temporary base. The *Chicago* landed first and Smith logged 10 hours 40 minutes flying time for the 835-mile flight. Nelson in the *New Orleans* put 11 hours 17 minutes in his log book.

Meanwhile, Locatelli, fearful of running into an iceberg or a mountain, decided to land and await clear weather. But instead of clearing, the weather got rougher and mountainous waves broke the *Dornier's* ailerons, stabilizer and elevators. The plane would never fly again. The four Italians, after floating for three days and nights were seasick and exhausted. They were finally located by the *Richmond* on August 24 and hauled aboard. Sailors punctured the plane's gas tanks, set it on fire and cast it adrift.

Meanwhile, messages had been flowing back and forth between Washington and the naval vessels. General Patrick decided that Wade and Ogden should not be denied the chance to participate further in the flight. He ordered the prototype World Cruiser, then at Langley Field, Virginia, to be flown to Pictou, Nova Scotia, where Wade and Ogden would meet the other fliers and continue with them to Seattle. It was to be named the *Boston II*.

Smith and Nelson still had another risky flight ahead of them. The next stop was Ivigtut, a small native village 150 miles farther up the west coast of Greenland where the cruiser *Milwaukee* was waiting with supplies for the flight to Labrador. Dodging ice floes in the harbor, they departed Fredricksdal on the morning of August 25. They flew for two hours along the bleak coast of Greenland through rain, snow and high winds that reminded them of the Alaskan williwaws. "Nearly every time we rounded a mountain," Nelson said, "a terrific gust of wind would strike from the shoulder of a fjord and knock us all over the sky."

When they landed beside the *Milwaukee* in a well protected harbor at Ivigtut, a ramp had been constructed along the beach for the planes to be pulled up out of the way of floating ice. The fliers then went aboard the ship to finalize plans for their final jump across the North Atlantic.

Realizing they had only one more long water flight ahead of them, they decided to eliminate as much risk as possible by changing engines. This had to be done in the open despite freezing rain. While this was being accomplished, the weather deteriorated further and takeoff was delayed until August 31st. The next stop was Icy Tickle, Labrador, 560 miles away.

Four U.S. Navy destroyers reported they were in position along the route. The two World Cruisers encountered heavy fog soon after takeoff, but it was short-lived and they emerged into

The Boston II, *the DWC prototype plane, was readied to send to Pictou, Nova Scotia, so that Wade and Ogden could contine the flight back to Seattle.* U.S. AIR FORCE MUSEUM

Capt. Lewis R. Knight, commandant of the Naval Air Station in Boston (left in straw hat) readies his pilots for the flight to Nova Scotia. In the middle is Lt. Victor C. Bertrandis and on the right is Lt. George C. MacDonald. U.S. AIR FORCE MUSEUM

clear weather that lasted until they neared the Labrador coast.

It was good flying weather and all was going well when the cold hand of Failure suddenly tried to claw us down, Smith reported. *We were two hundred miles from Labrador when our motor-driven pump failed, and five minutes later our wind-driven pump also gave out, making it necessary to turn on the reserve tank, containing fifty-eight gallons of gas, or enough for over two hours.*

I throttled down and shouted to Les that our one hope of maintaining the supply in the reserve tank and making shore lay in the wobble pump which is installed in all the planes for just such an emergency and is manipulated by hand. Les was already stripped to the waist. He laid hold of that handle and pumped with it for dear life.

Arnold pumped for nearly three hours without resting. His arm became numb, and an hour from Icy Tickle, they ran into a thick mist and a heavy 45-mile-an-hour head-wind that slowed them down considerably. Arnold made a sling with his belt, placed a handkerchief around his neck and pulled it with his other hand. Each time he thought he couldn't pump any more, he looked down at the cold ocean, thought about the consequences and resumed the tiresome task.

After nearly seven hours of flying, the two planes landed near the *Richmond* and *Laurence*. A motor launch took the fliers from their moorings to shore. Their greatest geographical obstacles were behind them now. They had flown a greater distance—20,090 miles—than had ever been flown by any other aerial expedition.

U. S. AVIATORS EXPECT TO TAKE TO AIR TODAY

By The Associated Press.
On Board U. S. S. Richmond at Ice Tickle, Labrador, Aug. 30.— Captain Thiesen, the American army meteorological expert who is noting weather conditions in connection with the world flight, tonight predicted favorable weather for the flight tomorrow. With the barometer rapidly rising, the fog overhanging the Labrador coast throughout today began scattering somewhat this evening.

Weather conditions this morning were fair at Ivigtut, but hazy along Davis strait. The news that another storm was heading up the coast toward this point and due Monday or Tuesday, will probably compel Lieutenants Lowell Smith and Erik Nelson to start tomorrow if the weather is possible for flying on the last leg of their transatlantic flight.

WORLD AVIATORS DELAY JUMP FROM GREENLAND

Atlantic Storm Reported to Be Moving Northward.

By The Associated Press.
On Board U. S. S. Richmond, Ice Tickle, Labrador, Aug. 27. — Further postponement of one day in the departure of the American army world flyers from Ivigtut, Greenland to Indian harbor, Labrador, was ordered this morning because of a storm which is reported to be moving north. Rear Admiral Thomas P. Magruder notified the vessels of the naval patrol that the flight had been postponed until Friday at the earliest.

Lieutenant Lowell H. Smith, commander of the world flight, messaged Rear Admiral Magruder that the work of installing new engines in the army planes was progressing favorably, although hampered somewhat by the rain Monday. The work, the message stated, probably would be completed by tonight and the aviators were planning to hop off for Indian harbor Friday.

Chapter 11
The Heroes
Return

The successful landing at Icy Tickle on August 31 was widely reported. It now seemed likely that the Americans would make their goal on the other side of the continent. When the fliers reached the shore, Smith as the flight's senior officer, was the first to step onto North American soil. Later, the six fliers were invited to the ship where Admiral Magruder read the following message from President Coolidge:

Your history-making flight has been followed with absorbing interest by your countrymen and your return to North American soil is an inspiration to the whole Nation. You will be welcomed back to the United States with an eagerness and enthusiasm that I am sure will compensate for the hardship you have undergone. Your countrymen are proud of you. Your branch of the Service realizes the honor you have won for it. My congratulations and heartiest good wishes go to you at this hour of your landing.

Secretary of War John W. Weeks sent radio messages to each of the fliers individually. The wire to Smith congratulated him for his "brav-

ery, hardihood, and modesty" and added that as leader of the flight, "I desire to say that your courage, skill and determination have shown you to be a fit successor to the great navigators of the Age of Discovery." General Patrick added his congratulations and said he would meet them in Boston.

Everyone worked on the two ships the next day and on September 2, although the weather was marginal, Smith decided they would leave for Hawkes Bay, Newfoundland, the next planned stop. Three hours from Icy Tickle, as they reached the Strait of Belle Isle, they ran into their old enemy, fog. They flew at wave-top level with their pontoons almost hitting the water; in one instance they narrowly missed colliding with a small steamer. When the fog abated, they ran into a stiff head-wind and it took six and a half hours to fly the 430 miles from Icy Tickle to Hawkes Bay. The destroyer *Osborne* was waiting and after refueling their planes, the fliers went aboard the ship for the night, the last they would spend aboard a naval vessel. Meanwhile, the *Richmond* transported Wade and Ogden to Pictou, Nova Scotia where their replacement plane, named the *Boston II*, was ready to join the flight.

The two DWCs arrive at Icy Tickle, Labrador, their first stop in North America since leaving Seattle in April. PICTORIAL HISTORIES

Smith was the first to set foot on North American soil. PICTORIAL HISTORIES

Lt. Wade holds the American flag at Pictou Harbor, Nova Scotia, on September 3, 1924. MUSEUM OF FLYING

Smith and Nelson took off from Hawkes Bay on the morning of September 3 and flew down the west coast of Newfoundland and across Cabot Strait and Cape Breton. As they neared Pictou Harbor, they saw the *Boston II* floating peacefully below. After landing, they refueled the planes and were taken ashore to experience the first of many official greetings, parades and receptions that were to follow. They were driven through crowd-packed, decorated streets behind bagpipers and school bands. The parade ended at a band platform where the fliers were introduced and each made "feeble, oratorical" comments, according to Nelson.

They planned to leave the next day for Boston, but the weather was rainy and windy. The three planes left at 11:15 a.m. on September 6, and just south of St. John, New Brunswick, ran into heavy fog. They dodged rocks and small islands for a while, then tried to climb over it but to no avail. Smith wisely decided it was too risky and led the other two planes to a sheltered cove at Casco Bay, off Point Mere, Maine.

Although they wanted to leave early on the 7th, a stiff headwind was blowing, and Smith decided they should take on more gas to ensure their getting to Boston. As they waited for the gas to be brought from a nearby town, ten deHavilland DH-4s, led by General Patrick and including Lts. Streett and Brown, two of the flight committee members, had flown up to escort them to Boston. The planes flew low and Smith held up a funnel and a gas can to let them know what was holding up their departure.

General Patrick, who had just earned his wings in 1923 at age 60, prepares to go up in his plane to greet the DWCs. PICTORIAL HISTORIES

After circling for a while, the DH-4s flew to Old Orchard, Maine, and landed on the beach to wait until they saw the Cruisers approaching.

The three Cruisers took off and flew to Boston without incident. Arriving over the airport, they saw fire boats in the harbor spouting streams of water, factories spewing smoke and warships firing salutes. As soon as they landed and went ashore, they were surrounded by hordes of people. General Patrick greeted them warmly, followed by the governor of Massachusetts, mayor of Boston, the assistant secretary of war and a host of other officials.

They were whisked into the city where the sidewalks were jammed with cheering throngs.

It was all totally unexpected, Smith said. *Of course, we hadn't seen a paper in Iceland, Greenland or Labrador. In fact, we had only glanced at a few foreign journals since leaving Seattle, so we hadn't the faintest idea there was going to be all this enthusiasm.*

When they arrived at the Boston Common, they were presented with a number of presents, including keys to the city, sabers, large Paul Revere bowls and watches. Afterwards, they were taken to the Copley-Plaza Hotel where they found dress uniforms and clean shirts in the closets, all neatly pressed, thanks to the advance officers.

We appreciated Boston's welcome, Smith said, *In fact, we reveled in it, having just come down from the bleak arctic; but it did make us feel uneasy and fidgety, for we still had over three thousand miles more to go.*

The planes could not be forgotten while their crews were being entertained. Air Service mechanics checked them over, and the pontoons were exchanged for wheels on September 7. The next day, they left Boston for Mitchel Field, Long Island, a major Air Service base. Escorted all the way by General Patrick and an entourage of other planes, they flew over the Statue of Liberty and the ships in New York harbor that were spewing smoke. Fire boats thrust huge streams of water upward in their traditional welcome salute. The three planes cut across Brooklyn to Long Island and were surprised to find the field filled with thousands of people. The Cruisers

The world fliers get a salute from military and civilians as they step ashore from the motor launch that brought them from their planes in the Boston harbor. U.S. AIR FORCE MUSEUM

A dinner was held for the fliers on September 7 at the Boston airport.
U.S. AIR FORCE MUSEUM

The three DWCs and an excort plane shown over New Haven, Connecticut.
PETER M. BOWERS COLLECTION

Lt. Smith supervising the removal of the DWC pontoons and installation of wheels in Boston for the remaining flight across the United States, September 7.
U.S. AIR FORCE MUSEUM

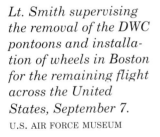

Lt. G.W. Goddard, left, piloted a special photographic plane across the country from Boston to California to record the historic journey. The aerial photographer was Lt. John A. Brockhorst.
U.S. AIR FORCE MUSEUM

The world fliers over New York City
on September 8.
U.S. AIR FORCE MUSEUM

The three DWCs with an escort led by General Patrick approaching New York City. U.S. AIR FORCE MUSEUM

Mitchel Field on Long Island was a major Air Service base. Thousands of people were lined up to greet their heroes. The top photo shows the DWCs over the field, the bottom shows them on the ground. Mitchel Field has now been turned into the Cradle of Aviation Museum. MUSEUM OF FLYING & U.S. AIR FORCE MUSEUM

The Prince of Wales, center, waits for the fliers to land at Mitchel Field.

PICTORIAL HISTORIES

The six airmen were welcomed at Mitchel Field and presented with engraved cigarette cases.
U.S. AIR FORCE MUSEUM

had to circle until the police cleared the field for their landing. As they taxied toward the parking ramp where General Patrick and the Prince of Wales were waiting, the crowds broke through the police lines and surrounded the planes.

For ten minutes we had to fight to keep souvenir hunters from pulling the planes to bits, Smith said. *Finally we milled through the mob to the reception stand, where Senator Wadsworth made a speech and presented us with the handsomest green–gold cigarette cases we had ever seen. On one face was a six-inch replica of a Douglas World Cruiser cut out of a block of platinum, and on the other an engraved map of the world showing the route of the flight and every place we had stopped.*

It was a bleak day on September 9, but it cleared sufficiently by 10 a.m. for the three Cruisers and their escorts, led by General Patrick, to depart for Washington where the president would be waiting. They headed south against a strong headwind that greatly reduced the ground speed of the planes. Eight miles north of Baltimore, the engine of the *New Orleans* suddenly quit, and Nelson had to make a forced landing in a pasture. There was no damage, and several of the escorting planes, including General Patrick's, landed beside him. Harding stayed behind to see if he could repair the engine while Patrick insisted Nelson continue to Washington in one of the escort planes.

After takeoff and still confronted by a stiff wind, the group landed at Aberdeen, Maryland, so that some of the short–range escorting DH-4s could refuel. They were now about three hours behind their announced schedule, but President Coolidge waited patiently during a downpour at Bolling Field. The planes landed, and the airmen received congratulations from the president, Mrs. Coolidge and Secretary of War Weeks.

The fliers remained in Washington for the next three days to participate in Defense Day ceremonies on September 12. They received hundreds of congratulatory messages including a laudatory cable from King George of England.

Meanwhile, the *New Orleans*, with a new engine, arrived at Bolling Field, and the three

Cruisers were flown over Washington and the Arlington National Cemetery where flowers were dropped on the Tomb of the Unknown Soldier, followed by a flight over the Defense Day parade on Pennsylvania Ave. The fliers then visited patients at the Army's Walter Reed Hospital and met with General Pershing whom they had visited previously in Paris.

When satisfactory weather reports were received on the 13th, the trio of planes left Bolling Field in mid–morning accompanied by several escort planes and headed west for McCook Field, Dayton, Ohio. Smith was leading and encountered very thick fog west of Harper's Ferry between Cumberland, Maryland and Uniontown, Pennsylvania.

They tried to climb over the fog, but it could not be topped so they hugged the tree tops. The escort planes departed, and Smith was able to follow a railroad while the other two planes followed in single file until they left the fog behind them.

They were intercepted by 20 planes near Columbus, Ohio, and escorted to McCook Field at Dayton. On the ground were about 50,000 people cheering and waving flags. As they emerged from their cockpits, they were swamped with flowers and gifts.

The stop at McCook was an opportunity for mechanics to check over every inch of the planes to determine exactly how much strain they had been able to take and determine if they were safe to continue. The men, too, were given rigid physical examinations and pronounced fit to continue, although they all admitted they were very tired.

Instead of the originally planned route across the Rocky Mountains via Cheyenne, Wyoming and Salt Lake City, Utah, with their high altitudes that would strain the capability of the Cruisers, Smith decided they would fly a southern route from Chicago. The three planes left McCook on September 15 and flew directly to the Chicago air mail field where they landed at mid–afternoon. They attended a large banquet that evening, and were presented with engraved cigarette cases filled with gold pieces.

They hoped to get off for Omaha, Nebraska, the next morning, but a heavy fog hung in all day long. They returned to the city and stayed overnight. They finally got off the next morning for Omaha, 460 miles away. They landed at

General Patrick presents Lt. Wade to President Coolidge, left, and Secretary of War Weeks, right, at Bolling field just outside Washington, D.C., on September 9. Looking on from the left are Arnold and Smith, from the right Wade and Ogden. Harding is not in the photograph. Below, the President is shaking Arnold's hand while Secretary Weeks looks on. Future president Herbert Hoover is in the background with his head turned. C.V. GLINES

Left to right: Smith, Wade and Nelson ride in a car during the National Defense Day celebration parade on September 12 in Washington, D.C.
U.S. AIR FORCE MUSEUM

The world fliers in front of the Chicago *at McCook Field in Dayton, Ohio. From Left: Major Currie (not crew), Smith, Ogden, Nelson, Wade, Harding and Arnold.*
U.S. AIR FORCE MUSEUM

In most every city where the world fliers stopped, crowds converged around the aircraft, sometimes keeping the crews from servicing them. This crowd is at the Maywood Airmail field, just outside Chicago, Illinois.
U.S. AIR FORCE MUSEUM

Welcome Home

victorious bird-men to the "Birth Place of the Airplane"

To you conquerors of the World's uncharted aerial sea

Lieutenants:

Lowell H. Smith

Eric H. Nelson

Leigh Wade

Leslie T. Arnold

John Harding, Jr.

H. H. Ogden

all Dayton pours forth the warmest greetings of her heart, born of an understanding of the trials of flying. What you have endured, we shall probably never know, but posterity will never cease to recall what you have accomplished.

Even while we have watched distance annihilated under the wings of the airplane upon this continent, by spanning it from dawn to dusk you have linked by air the Nations of the World bringing all mankind within the scope of aerial navigation.

As you near the end of your voyage, our emotions are only restrained by your wishes. We await your return to the International Air Races to fittingly express our full appreciation of what you have done.

The City of Dayton

The Dayton Chamber of Commerce

The Dayton Chapter A.A.A.

CHICAGO COMMERCE

Published Weekly by THE CHICAGO ASSOCIATION of COMMERCE

WORLD FLYERS
OFFICIAL PROGRAM

the Jarvis Offutt Army Field at Fort Crook amid mass confusion. Soldiers moved in to protect the planes and keep the people from touching them. Next morning, September 17, they flew 110 miles to St. Joseph, Missouri, where they attended a civic club luncheon and then left for Muskogee, Oklahoma, through heavy rain squalls. Twenty-five thousand people were waiting there with a thunderous welcome at Hat Box Field. They had another banquet that night where they received golden medallions commemorating their visit.

It was on to Love Field, Dallas, Texas, on September 19 against a stiff headwind and rain where the reception was the same as before: large crowds, a big banquet, and more unexpected gifts commemorating the visit. The intention was to fly non-stop from Dallas to El Paso, but the three planes landed at Sweetwater because the *Boston II* had oil pump trouble. Repairs were made quickly, and the flight continued to the Air Service field at Fort Bliss at dusk. It had been a long day with 9 hours 24 minutes of flying time.

A flight to Tucson, Arizona, was next for an overnight stay and then on to San Diego where the fliers had started from before proceeding to Seattle, the official starting point. San Diegans considered their city as the flight's origin and had been preparing a homecoming party for weeks. They arrived early and thirty escort planes hurriedly flew out to shepherd them to a landing. That evening, the fliers were given a reception at the San Diego stadium which was attended by 35,000 people. Again, the six men were presented with expensive gifts.

Meanwhile, mechanics changed the engines on all three planes. On the 23rd, they left San Diego for Santa Monica, escorted by a large number of planes from the nearby naval air station and Rockwell Field. The three Cruisers flew over Los Angeles and landed at Clover Field where the crowd was estimated at more than one hundred thousand people.

All around us was a heavy line of guards, Smith said. *As we crawled out of our cockpits, the crowd went wild. With a roar, they knocked down the fence. They knocked down the police. they knocked down the soldiers. They knocked us down. They tried to pull our ships apart for souvenirs, but somehow we fought them off.*

The crowd was so unruly that the fliers couldn't refuel or do any work on their planes as they always did after a flight. That night they went to Hollywood and stayed at the Christie Hotel where the manager had affixed an engraved plaque on each door with their names saying that they had occupied the room upon completion of the world flight.

The possibility of flying mishaps was not over. On the way to San Francisco on September 25, Wade in the *Boston II* had to land south of the city briefly with engine trouble while the other two planes landed at Crissy Field. That evening they were each presented with a check for $1,250 by the city's mayor at a large reception. Wade's plane had to have an engine change which delayed the takeoff for Eugene, Oregon, until the 27th. It was a repeat of the previous landings with a huge crowd waiting for them, greetings by local dignitaries and a large reception that evening.

The itinerary called for the last leg of the flight to Seattle, but all three planes landed at Vancouver Barracks briefly because of engine trouble on the *Boston II*. The trouble was soon remedied, and they left on the last hop to their official starting point to complete their mission. They landed three abreast at the Sand Point Field so that each plane would finish the flight simultaneously. The official time of landing was 1:28 p.m. Pacific time, September 28, 1924.

A huge dinner was held at the Chicago Beach Hotel on September 16 for the world heroes.

Citizens of San Diego, California, present a silver tea service to the world fliers. MUSEUM OF FLYING

The Chicago *returns to Clover Field in Santa Monica on September 23. Many considered Clover Field the actual start of the Round-the-World Flight.* MUSEUM OF FLYING

The Chicago *lands at Crissy Field on September 25.* U.S. AIR FORCE MUSEUM

When the planes reached Crissy Field at the Presidio of San Francisco, one hundred thousand people greeted them. U.S. AIR FORCE MUSEUM

"Miss San Francisco" giving Commander Smith the official kiss of welcome while the others nervously await their turns.
PICTORIAL HISTORIES

Left to right: Nelson, Smith, Harding and Arnold in San Francisco.
U.S. AIR FORCE MUSEUM

Chapter 12
Mission
Accomplished

There were an estimated 50,000 people waiting on the Sand Point airfield for the triumphant landing. Among those greeting the six airmen was Major Martin whom they had last seen before his near-tragic flight in Alaska. There were greetings from local dignitaries and presentations of valuable mementos. Then began a whirlwind of press interviews, receptions and speeches.

Flight commander Smith talks to Seattle Mayor Brown at the end of the journey. PICTORIAL HISTORIES

The enthusiasm all along the coast was really remarkable, Smith reported. *Couples arranged their marriages to coincide with the termination of the World Flight and there was a fashion for a time of wearing beauty patches cut in the silhouette of a Douglas Cruiser. They were even naming babies for us.*

The following afternoon, Seattle friends took us out to Sand Point Field, where Les Arnold's sister, Mrs. Francis L. Cole, unveiled a monument commemorating Seattle as the official starting point and end of the first World Flight. It was a granite shaft fifteen feet high with a

21 Gun Salute To Greet U.S. World Flyers

SYMBOLIC of the honors heaped upon them at home and abroad America's successful globe girdlers will receive the highest possible honor from their brothers in arms when their planes settle at Sand Point field today.

A twenty-one gun salute, flaming from the muzzles of a battery of French 75's manned by picked men of Battery C, 146th Field Artillery, will commence as soon as Lieutenant Smith's trio of ships is sighted.

Reserved for more than 100 years as an honor to be paid only to present and former presidents, sovereigns of foreign nations and members of royal houses, the twenty one gun salute has for the first time been accorded to those of lesser rank.

A DWC landing at Sand Point Field in Seattle.
PETER M. BOWERS

Seattle Post-Intelligencer

VOL. LXXXVI. NO. 140. SEATTLE, MONDAY, SEPTEMBER 29, 1924. TWENTY-FOUR PAGES. DAILY

ALL SEATTLE SEES WORLD FLIGHT E...

Maj. Martin In Tears As He Is Cheere...

CITY GIVES OVATION TO U.S. FLYERS

CROWDS WELCOME FLYERS HOME

THOUSANDS UNITE IN MIGHTY WELCOME FOR TRIUMPHANT BIRDMEN

Huge Crowd at Sand Point Thunders Forth Greeting to Intrepid Flyers: All Seattle Opens Arms to Sky Pioneers, Heroes of Nation, As Chapter In History Written

By Fred Niendorff

| 1 KILLED, 2 HURT | Coolidge Will Urge | MRS. ROGERS ...ES GRANDSON |

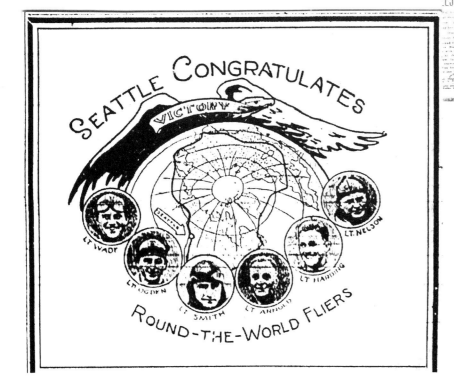

SEATTLE CONGRATULATES
VICTORY
ROUND-THE-WORLD FLIERS

LT. WADE
LT. OGDEN
LT. SMITH
LT. ARNOLD
LT. HARDING
LT. NELSON

New York American

September 6, 1924.

Seattle Post-Intelligencer, *September 17, 1924.*

AVIATION MONUMENT COMMEMORATES AIR TRIP AROUND GLOBE

Shaft Erected and Dedicated at Seattle; Flyers to Enter Races.

By The Associated Press.

Seattle, Sept. 29.—Plans were being made tonight by six United States army lieutenants, who completed the first circumnavigation of the globe here yesterday, to leave Seattle at 9:30 o'clock tomorrow morning to attend the Pulitzer airplane races at Dayton, Ohio.

A program of addresses, concluded with a dedicatory talk by United States Senator Wesley L. Jones, preceeded the unveiling of a monument today at Sandpoint aviation field, erected in commemoration of the first around-the-world airplane flight. The monument was erected by Mrs. Frances Cole of Spokane, Wash., sister of Lieutenant Leslie P. Arnold, mechanic for Lieutenant Lowell H. Smith, commander of the flight. Mrs. Cora Arnold, mother of Lieutenant Arnold, was present at the ceremony.

Made of Polished Granite.

The polished granite column is 15 feet high, three feet wide at the base and tapers to two feet in width at the top. Bronze wings on the top of a model of the globe symbolize a bird alighting at the end of a long flight. It was designed and modeled by Victor Alonzo Lewis, Seattle sculptor.

"We dedicate this shaft to tell the ages of their achievement," Senator Jones said in his address. "Let us hope that the journey which began and ended where this monument stands will intensify the interest of the American people in air navigation, making it a blessing to civilization and put an end to war and waste."

Each Flyer Speaks.

Each of the six flyers appeared on the speakers' stand and gave a short address. Major Frederick L. Martin, former commander of the flight called on to talk, praised his comrades in a voice husky with emotion and urged utmost support for aviation.

The speeches by the flyers at Sandpoint were the second on the day's program as they were asked earlier to give their opinions of the flight at a luncheon given under the auspices of the Seattle Chamber of Commerce.

"The hardest part of the trip was leaving Seattle, April 6, for Seattle, knowing that we would have to go all around the world to get here," said Lieutenant Smith in his first address.

Talking Harder Than Flying.

"It's harder to talk to you than it is to fly around the world," was Lieutenant Leigh Wade's comment.

"I'm the worst talker of the bunch," said Lieutenant Erik Nelson. "I've never made a talk before except when I was called upto to speak in Shanghai, China. We all appreciate the help given us by the air service organization in Washington, the United States coast guard, the bureau of fisheries and the navy."

With the greatest of their worries over with — speeches, as Lieutenant Smith expressed it after the cere-

Mr. and Mrs. Harding stop at the Sand Point monument in 1929. U.S. AIR FORCE MUSEUM

PARADE LINE OF MARCH FOR TODAY GIVEN

Party Will Form at City Hall Park At 9:45 A. M. for Trip To Sand Point; Police Escort

Today's itinerary for the world flyers' official reception committee and details concerning the parade from City Hall Park to the New Washington hotel were announced by the Chamber of Commerce yesterday as follows:

Form in line at City Hall Park at 9:45 a. m. and drive in line East to Fourth Avenue, north on Fourth Avenue to Madison Street; east on Madison to Madison Street dock, Lake Washington, where party will board Yacht Aquila or Eagle Boat for Sand Point.

Cars will be parked, on arrival at end of Madison Street, under police direction, until return of party from Sand Point.

On returning to Madison Street dock from Sand Point, cars will form in line again and parade east on Madison Street to Boulevard; thence north on Boulevard to Twenty-fourth Avenue; turn left to Crescent Drive ,and continue through to Galer Street; west on Galer to Volunteer Park.

Only official cars will be allowed to enter the park. All other cars will park on adjacent streets, outside of park.

Official cars, on entering park, will follow police escort on main roadway and maintaining their line, will park on roadway within the park.

At the close of ceremonies, official cars will continue through main roadway of park and east to Broadway, followed through the Galer Street entrance by all cars that have not entered the park, which will fall in line as soon as the official cars get under headway. Following police escort, parade will turn south on Broadway to Pine; west on Pine to Third, south on Third to City Hall Park and Yesler Way; west on Yesler to Second; north on Second to Washington Hotel, where

---

globe at the top surmounted by a pair of bronze wings. On one side was a bronze plate bearing our names and the dates of our departure and return. We had certainly never expected to see our names on a monument until we were under it.

Their mission completed, the fliers wondered what they would be asked to do next. They didn't have to wait long. General Patrick sent a telegram instructing them to attend the International Air Races in Dayton.

We were delighted, Smith recalled, *because we thought, oh, well, the flight's over and tomorrow the country will have forgotten about it and us, so on our way to Dayton we'll just catch up on lost sleep. But we were wrong.*

They boarded the railroad and headed east. Instead of getting to rest, the train was delayed at each stop for ceremonies, and they were presented with mementos varying from silk neckerchiefs to live animals. Stacks of letters, most of them from young women, were always waiting when the train pulled into a station. When they finally got to Dayton, they were met by Orville Wright who congratulated them on their achievement. They were the focal point for photographers and reporters at the Dayton races and took part in the air race program.

When the air races were over, General Patrick directed them to return to Seattle and fly the Cruisers back across the continent so decisions could be made about their disposal. They returned via Los Angeles and El Paso where the flight split up. The *Boston II* and *New Orleans* went to San Antonio, Houston, and New Orleans, while the *Chicago* went to St. Louis; there Smith and Arnold entrained for Chicago where they were swamped with invitations to luncheons and dinners. They were completely surprised at a huge gathering in the Chicago Auditorium when the mayor of Chicago presented both of them with a Packard sedan.

The three planes were flown to McCook Field in Dayton to await a decision on their disposition. The fliers then went to Washington to meet with General Patrick and make out their official reports. A few months later, Congress voted to award the six fliers the Distinguished Service Medal.

At Seattle the world fliers say good-bye and start east for their next adventure.
PICTORIAL HISTORIES

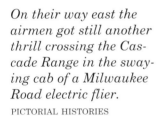

On their way east the airmen got still another thrill crossing the Cascade Range in the swaying cab of a Milwaukee Road electric flier.
PICTORIAL HISTORIES

A question arose in Washington as to the proper disposition of the *Chicago* and *New Orleans*. Chicago's Mayor William E. Dever requested that the plane be awarded to the city of Chicago as a permanent exhibit. Other cities requested that the pilots and planes visit for public display but, to avoid adverse comment, the Secretary of War decided that the *Chicago* would be placed in the Smithsonian Institution in Washington and the *New Orleans* at the Air Service Museum at McCook Field. Neither plane would be flown again or loaned for expositions and air shows. Today, the *Chicago* can be seen in the Smithsonian's National Air & Space Museum. The *New Orleans*, formerly at the Air Force Museum in Dayton, Ohio, is now in the Museum of Flying at Santa Monica, California. The *Boston II* was

used for testing but was eventually scrapped in 1932.

Lt. Lowell Smith, as the flight leader, prepared a report of the incidents that occurred on each leg. He praised the work of the World Flight Committee for their effective planning, and the assistance of the U.S. Navy between the Kurile Islands and Calcutta as well as the Light Cruiser Division from Scotland across the North Atlantic to Boston. The help rendered by the two Coast Guard cutters in the Aleutian Islands was also highly commended, as was the Bureau of Fisheries.

In every Nation or country or wherever a landing was made, the inhabitants, if any, were anxious to do everything within their power to assist the flight, Smith added. *The*

On the way back east in November 1924 the DWCs landed at Kelly Field in San Antonio, Texas, on the 6th. Pilot Lt. Erik Nelson and Lt. Harding, in the rear cockpit of the New Orleans, are being greeted by Col. James E. Fechet, commander of the field.   Below, the Boston II is being stopped by three army ground crew at Kelly Field. Neither the DWCs nor any other airplane had brakes in 1924, so a long field or ground personnel were needed. The Boston II ended up at Kelly Field where it was scrapped in 1932.

Japanese Air Service, the Royal Air Force and the French Air Force were of greater service to the flight than other countries, this most likely being due to the fact that their air strength was much larger.

The Danish Government Coast Guard Service turned the Island Falk over to the flight. While in Greenland, the Island Falk was used to establish the emergency base at Fredricksdal, near Cape Farewell, and was of the utmost value in the success of the flight at this point.

Smith reserved his highest compliments for the advance officers for the "untiring and efficient manner" in which they fulfilled their duties under the most trying hardships.

These officers had to establish lines of communication by radio, ship supplies to isolated islands and cities, establish all supply bases, gain information for the flight at each expected landing place, select and appoint a responsible local agent at each stop; then after the flight passed, they were charged with the duties of taking care of all the financial obligations and returning all surplus supplies to regular Air Service Supply Depots by the best transportation available. They were exposed to many hardships in the northern waters and sickness through the tropical countries, but, in every case, successfully accomplished their mission, overcoming all obstacles.

The six world fliers pose with adventurer Lowell Thomas after the trip. Left to right: Arnold, Harding, Nelson, Wade, Smith, Lowell Thomas, Ogden and Mrs. Corliss Moseley, secretary to the aviators. Thomas would publish the first complete account of the journey in his 1925 book The First World Flight.
JIM RUOTSALA

Erik Nelson, engineering officer for the flight, submitted a detailed report about the condition of the planes, including the changes he had recommended during their construction. He discussed the flight progress in chronological order about the maintenance and repairs that had to be made at many stops. He was especially complimentary about the construction of the planes.

Lt. Leigh Wade, Supply Officer for the flight, submitted a report on how the aircraft and engine parts had survived shipment to the various distribution points. He said there were instances when supplies stored at many of the bases could have been sold locally after the aircraft passed through for a profit, rather than be shipped back to the Air Service.

Lt. Leslie Arnold had been appointed the Finance Officer for the flight and had been given $17,000 in Tokyo to handle payments that had to be made en route. He said it had been difficult at times to pay all charges such as hotel bills when they passed through so many different countries with so many different kinds of currency at different exchange rates. The pilot of each plane had been given $1,000 at the start of the flight to be used as an emergency fund.

Smith submitted a classified appendix to the main report. He noted that the six of them were received very courteously by the Japanese, especially by the school children who attended their landings by the thousands. Smith thought that the Japanese were sincere in their enthusiasm but that there was an underlying feeling against the American government. He commented, "This may have been due to the unrest among the Japanese people caused by the Japanese Exclusion Act which had been passed only two weeks previous."

With the successful conclusion of this epic flight, it might be said that aviation had proven itself and come of age. The world had been circumnavigated, a feat that many had believed impossible. Aircraft seemed to fly ever higher, faster and farther with each passing day. The time has come now to look back and honor the men whose personal courage and fortitude triumphed over unforeseen obstacles that lesser men would not have attempted to overcome.

Other World Cruisers

The Round-the-World Flight was such a success with the U.S. Air Service that they purchased six additional world cruisers from the Douglas Company. They were to be used as observation aircraft. Initially designated as DOS (Douglas Observation Seaplane), the aircraft, numbered 24-2 through 24-7, retained the interchangeable wheel/float undercarriage but had its fuel capacity reduced to 110 gallons. Twin .30 cal. machine guns were mounted in the rear cockpit. They were redesignated O-S and were operated by the 2nd Observation Squadron off of Kindley Field on the island of Corregidor for the Philippine Aviation Department. Their final disposition is unknown.

MUSEUM OF FLYING

Monaco was the only country to honor the world fliers with a commemorative stamp forty years later in 1964. A U.S. Postal Service committee turned down the request for a commemorative 50th anniversary stamp as not being of sufficient public interest.
C.V. GLINES

The Story of a Great American Achievement

THE FIRST WORLD FLIGHT

As told by Lieut. John T. ("Smiling Jack") Harding

ILLUSTRATED WITH WONDERFUL MOVING AND STILL PICTURES

TOUR MANAGEMENT ELBERT A. WICKES

442 LITTLE BLDG. BOSTON, MASS.

"High Spots" of the Lecture

Origin of the plan—The story of the girl on celluloid carried around the world by the Fliers, as a goddess of good fortune—The first "hop-off" —the six lucky "monkeys" accompanying the Fliers—Formal farewell to old Mount Shasta.

Into the Unknown—Through fog, rain and snow in Alaska—The first catastrophe—The un-lucky rabbit's foot—Out over the ice and for the first time—Through the Alaskan snows fifty feet above the sea—Fighting the "Woolies" of Dutch Harbor—Goodbye parachutes, life-belts and other personal safeguards—Battling the gales of Beh-ring Sea—Adventures with the Bolsheviki. Ad-ventures with the hairy men of Japan and the Geisha girls in Tokyo—Battling a typhoon and landing in a stormy sea. The first aerial crossing of the Yellow Sea.

Reception in Shanghai over a carpet of roses strewn by American girls—Forced landing in a lagoon—Begging food at a native temple—A night in a plane in unknown waters—Crossing Marco Polo's land of the golden Chersonese—Over the land of the White Elephant and the Malay jungles —Interesting reactions of natives—On the road to Mandalay — Dysentery, Buddhism, B u r m e s e maidens and black cheroots.

Passing a British World Flier—Encounters with natives of eastern India—Wild buffalo— "The City of Dreadful Night"—Strange Hindu customs—The first aerial stowaway—Across the Kipling country—Through intense heat and a battle with a desert sandstorm—Sheiks and she-bas—Engine trouble over the Sind desert, where a forced landing would have meant death—Along the shore line of the Arabian sea—Trailing camel caravans—Across romantic Persia to the Garden of Eden—Modern adventures in Bagdad.

Narrow escape near Babylon and Ur of the Chaldees—Crossing the Arabian desert—Flirting with death in the gorges between Mesopotamia and Anatolia—A visit to the Troglodytes of Cappodocia who live in thousand-year-old sky-scrapers—Over the Blue Danube—Across the old Hindenburg line into gay Paree—Welcome kisses from American girls at Croydon—The bonnie Highlands of Scotland from the sky—Nelson lost in fog and the tragic sinking of the Boston.

Iceland to Greenland, all in the day's work— Fighting blizzards and icebergs—Giving the Eskimos a thrill—A near failure on the eve of accomplishment—Troubles in Maine—Triumphal flight into the United States—Interesting reac-tions upon landing on American soil—Ordeal by banquet—Dodging the flappers—Significance of the Flight in the eyes of the world—Official "de-mobilization."

Masonic Temple
MONDAY, FEB. 23, 1925

4 p. m. For Children, Admission 25 cents

8:15 p. m. For Masons and friends, Admission 50 cents

RICKENBACKER MOTOR COMPANY

DETROIT, MICH.
April 28, 1925.

CABLE ADDRESS "RICKO"

E. V. RICKENBACKER
VICE-PRESIDENT

Mr. Jack Harding,
Cleveland,   Ohio.

My dear Jack:-

It was with genuine pleasure that the writer enjoyed a
few moments of renewing old acquaintances during your
visit to Detroit, and my only regret is that your time
was so limited.

May I take this opportunity of congratulating you, as
well as all other Members of the "Round-the-World" Flight
on the hardships encountered during this epochal event,
which were so aptly portrayed, as were the beauties and
unusual events, in the Movies and Slides shown while here.

It is unfortunate, indeed, that every citizen of the
United States will not have an opportunity of seeing
these photographs and hearing your very interesting, as
well as educational discourse on this remarkable flight,
as I am sure if they were able to, they would all feel
as the writer does, that it was an opportunity of a life
time.

Most sincerely,

Vice-President,
RICKENBACKER MOTOR COMPANY.

EVR/s.

WESTERN UNION TELEGRAM

Form 1204

CLASS OF SERVICE	SYMBOL
Telegram	
Day Letter	Blue
Night Message	Nite
Night Letter	N L

NEWCOMB CARLTON, PRESIDENT   GEORGE W. E. ATKINS, FIRST VICE-PRESIDENT

RECEIVED AT SANTA MONICA, CAL., PHONE 21039
6X M 59 BLUE

SANTA MONICA CALIF 200P SEPT 23 1924

LIEUT JOHN HARDING
        CLOVER FIELD SANTA MONICA CALIF
CONGRATULATIONS TO YOU MASTER AIR MEN OF THE WORLD ON YOUR WONDERFUL
ACHIEVEMENT STOP IT LOOKS AS THOUGH MY PREDICTION FOR CIRCLING THE
EARTH IN EIGHTY DAYS WILL SOON BE MET STOP WHEN YOU TOGETHER WITH
DONALD DOUGLAS FLY TO THE LAND IN WHICH I NOW RESIDE I WILL BE MUCH
PLEASED TO HEAR THE STORY OF YOUR TRIP
        JULES VERNE
            210P

*This telegram, of course, is a joke as Jules
Verne, author of the famous novel* Around
the World in Eighty Days *died in 1905.*

Joseph Anthony Atchison is shown working on a massive sculpture at his Hollywood studio in 1925. Five of the fliers stand behind their likeness. PICTORIAL HISTORIES

The world fliers ready for display at the Smithsonian Museum in Washington, D.C. It stands six feet high and seven feet wide with a bust of each of the fliers. Above them hovers the spirit of aviation. This sculpture was on display with the Chicago *at the National Air and Space Museum for many years but has now been put into storage.*

U.S. AIR FORCE MUSEUM

Secretary of War Dwight F. Davis decorating three of the eight Round-the-World fliers in the office of the Secretary of War, Washington, D.C., April 27, 1925. Davis pins the award on Maj. Martin. To Martin's left are Lt. Wade, Lt. Arnold, and Maj. Gen. Mason Patrick. In the rear are Brig. Gen. James E. Fecht, Brig. Gen. Wm. E. Gillmore, Lt. Col. James A. Mars, and Maj. H. A. Dargue.

The Boston II *is shown at Kelly Field, San Antonio, Texas, in 1925. It was flown back to McCook field but was finally scrapped at Kelly Field in May 1932.*

Nelson and Harding in front of the New Orleans *at Santa Monica, 1943.*

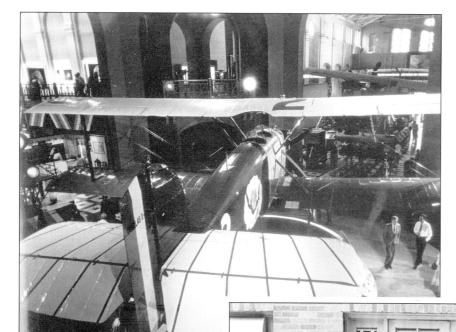

The Chicago *on display in the Smithsonian Institution Museum in the 1950s. It was moved to the National Air and Space Museum in 1971 where it is still on display.* C.V. GLINES

Years after the flight, five of the world fliers got together at Santa Monica. From the left: Martin, Nelson, Ogden, Harding and Arnold. U.S. AIR FORCE MUSEUM

Maj. Gen. and Mrs. Leigh Wade view the Chicago *at its display area in the National Air and Space Museum on the 50th anniversary of the flight, April 1974.* C.V. GLINES

Sometime after 1925 the New Orleans *was donated to the Los Angeles County Museum. In 1957 it was put on long-term loan to the U.S. Air Force Museum at Wright-Patterson AFB, Ohio. These photos show it stripped down for shipment to Ohio, the rebuilding but not restoration, and the display area at the museum. In 1988 the plane was brought back to its original home in Santa Monica and is on display at the Museum of Flying at the old Clover Field site.* PETER M. BOWERS COLLECTION VIA U.S. AIR FORCE MUSEUM

Appendix

FOR RELEASE March 9th, 1924 and thereafter.

WAR DEPARTMENT
OFFICE OF THE CHIEF OF AIR SERVICE
WASHINGTON

U. S. ARMY'S AROUND-THE-WORLD FLIGHT

The following official information includes a resumé of the revised plans for the Army's around-the-world flight and gives the detailed route with schedule of dates that planes are expected to reach each stop.

The itinerary has been chosen after a careful study of all available information to be obtained on the countries throughout which the flight will pass.

DIFFICULTIES

The crossing of the Atlantic and Pacific Oceans will present the greatest difficulty to be encountered in the flight around the world. It is impractical to attempt either the flight across the Atlantic or the Pacific Oceans, except by way of Iceland and Greenland in the Atlantic, and the Aleutian Islands in the Pacific. Long water flights are not considered practical with the present equipment and facilities available to carry out the intricate navigation problems which would attend such an undertaking. It is also felt that a successful flight over the present route would not only be a greater accomplishment, but would afford an opportunity to open up realms to aviation that heretofore remained closed.

PONTOONS

The preparation of landing fields over the entire route for the flight round-the-world would be highly impractical, both from the standpoint of expense and from the standpoint of time available for this work. Therefore, it has been decided that the portion of the route from Seattle, Washington, to Calcutta, India, will be flown in ships equipped for water landing, as will be that portion of the route from Brough (Hull), England, to the United States. The rest of the flight will be covered in land planes.

Since the successful accomplishment of this vast undertaking depends almost entirely upon weather conditions, the time of year chosen for the start and the schedule planned were based entirely upon the necessity of taking advantage of the most favorable flying conditions along the most hazardous and isolated sections of the route.

THE HOP OFF

Starting from Los Angeles, California, on March 15th, the flight will proceed by way of Sacramento to Seattle. Leaving this point about April 1st, it will proceed along the following route:

NOTE: THE POINTS UNDERLINED ARE STOPS WHERE PONTOONS WILL BE USED.

Stops indicated by * Main supply bases
Stops indicated by # Minor supply bases.

U-669-A,Rev.2/29/24, A.S.

FIRST DIVISION

	Statute Miles	Estimated Date of Arrival
*Seattle, Wash.		March 24, 1924.
Prince Rupert, B.C.	650	April 1, 1924.
#Sitka, Alaska	300	
Cordova, "	475	April 3, 1924
Seward, Alaska	135	
Chignik, Alaska	450	April 5, 1924
*Dutch Harbor, Unalaska, Alaska	400	April 8, 1924
Nazan, Island of Atka	350	
#Chicagoff, Island of Attu	530	April 11, 1924

SECOND DIVISION

Kashiwabara Bay, Paramushiru, Kuriles	860	April 14, 1924
Bettobu, Yetorofu, Kuriles	510	April 15, 1924
Minato, N.E. Coast Honshu, Japan	475	April 17, 1924
(Aomori to be used as Supply Base)		
Kasumiga Ura, Japanese Air Station	395	April 22, 1924
*(Yokohoma to be used as Supply Base)		
Osaka, Japan, Japanese Air Station	360	April 26, 1924
Kagoshima, Kyushu, Japan	380	April 27, 1924
#(Nagasake to be used as a Supply Base)		

THIRD DIVISION

#Shanghai, China	610	May 5, 1924.
Amoy, China	555	
Hong Kong, China	300	May 8, 1924
Haiphong, French Indo-China	500	May 10, 1924
Tourane, French Indo-China	395	May 13, 1924
#Saigon, French Indo-China	530	May 17, 1924
Bangkok, Siam	675	May 19, 1924
Rangoon, Burma	450	May 22, 1924
Akyab, Burma	445	May 26, 1924
*Calcutta, India	400	May 28, 1924

FOURTH DIVISION

Allahabad, India	475	June 4, 1924
Delhi, India	380	June 6, 1924
Multan, India	425	June 7, 1924
#Karachi, India	475	June 9, 1924
Charbar, Persia	330	June 10, 1924
Bandar, Abbas, Persia	330	June 11, 1924
Bushire, Persia	400	June 13, 1924
#Bagdad, Irak	475	June 14, 1924
Aleppo, Syria	480	June 16, 1924
Konia, Turkey	285	June 17, 1924
*San Stefano, Turkey	300	June 19, 1924

FIFTH DIVISION

Bucharest, Roumania	290	June 23, 1924
Belgrade, Serbia	290	June 24, 1924
Budapest, Hungary	220	June 25, 1924
#Vienna, Austria	140	June 26, 1924
Strassbourg, France	400	June 27, 1924
Paris, France	250	June 28, 1924
*London, England	225	July 1, 1924

SIXTH DIVISION

	Statute Miles	Estimated Date of arrival
*Brough, (Hull) England	155	July 2, 1924
Kirkwall, Orkney Islands	370	July 10, 1924
#Thorshavn, Faroe Islands	275	July 12, 1924
Hofn Hornafjord, Iceland	260	July 13, 1924
#Reykjavik, Iceland	339	July 14, 1924
#Ahgmagsalik, Greenland	500	July 16, 1924
#Ivigtut, Greenland	500	July 18, 1924
Indian Harbor, Laborador	572	July 24, 1924
Cartwright Harbor, Laborador	40	July 26, 1924
Hawkes Bay, Newfoundland	290	July 28, 1924
Pictou Harbor, Nova Scotia	420	July 30, 1924
Boston, Mass.	520	August 2, 1924.
Mitchel Field, L.I., N.Y.	175	August 8, 1924
Washington, D.C.	220	August 10, 1924

Unless the flight moves throughout the entire route with a regularity which will allow it to pass through the danger zones during a given period the eventual success of it is doubtful.

Air Service officials are confident that with anything at all like an even break of luck all of the four planes will return to their starting point on schedule. Previous attempts to encircle the globe by air have been unsuccessful but the forthcoming attempt of the American Army has been so carefully planned in every detail that success is practically assured.

TO AVOID BAD WEATHER

The following schedule of movement will allow the minimum of bad weather taking into consideration the fact the flight must be completed within a period of six months at the longest.

> 1st Division - Seattle to the Island of Attu, including the first portion of 2nd Division (through the Kurile Islands)- April and May.
>
> 2nd Division - Japan proper and Chosen - May and June
>
> 3rd Division - Kagoshima, Japan to Calcutta - May, June, July.
>
> 4th Division - Calcutta to Constantinople - June, July, August
>
> 5th Division - Constantinople to London - July, August
>
> 6th Division - London to the United States - August, and September

It should be borne in mind that should any condition relating either to weather conditions, or the facilities for landing, come to the attention of the advance officers, which has not been foreseen by this office, and which will in the opinion of the advance officers entail undue danger, they will immediately communicate with office stating the circumstances clearly, by the most rapid means of communication available to them.

WHERE ENGINES WILL BE CHANGED

It is expected that the flyers will arrive about April 28th at Kasumigaura on Choshi Ko, where motors will be changed. Calcutta, India, will be reached probably about May 24th; here new wings will be fitted, new motors installed and pontoons replaced with landing gears. At San Stefano, is a Turkish airdrome just outside Constantinople. The flyers hope to reach this port about June 16th and motors will be changed there if necessary. Arriving at Brough near Hull, England, about July 7th, the engines will be changed again for the last time and landing wheels replaced with pontoons for the final and perhaps most dangerous lap, the hop across the northern Atlantic by way of Iceland and Greenland.

The following personnel has been selected to set out from Los Angeles, California, March 15th, in four U. S. Army Air Service World Cruisers:

FLIGHT PERSONNEL

Major Frederick L. Martin of Indiana, Flight Commander; Lieut. Erik Nelson, who was born at Stockholm, Sweden, Engineer Officer; Lieut. Lowell H. Smith of California; Lieut. Leigh Wade of Michigan; Lieut. Leslie P. Arnold of Connecticut, and Lieut. LaClair D. Schulze of California, alternates, all of whom are pilots. The mechanicians are Reserve Lieut. John Harding, Jr., of Tennessee; Technical Sergeant Arthur H. Turner of California; Staff Sergeant Henry H. Ogden of Mississippi and Staff Sergeant Alva L. Harvey of Texas.

PLANNING BOARD

Detailed plans for the flight were worked out by the following committee, under the direction of the Chief of the Training Division of the Air Service:

Captain William F. Volant, Transportation and Finance;
Lieut. St. Clair Streett, Route Maps and Organization;
Lieut. Robert J. Brown, Jr., Co-ordination;
Lieut. Erik Nelson, Equipment and Engineering;
Lieut. Elmer E. Adler, Supply;
Lieut. Clarence E. Crumrine, Advance Officer.

PURPOSE

The chief purposes of this flight are:

1. To gain for the Air Service additional experience in long distance flying and particularly in the supply problem connected therewith.

2. To demonstrate the feasibility of establishing an airway around the world.

3. To test existing flying equipment under the extremes of climatic conditions.

4. To secure for the United States, the birthplace of aeronautics, the honor of being the first country to encircle the world entirely by air.

Note: Total miles flown - 26,445
      Flying time - Chicago - 363 hours, 7 minutes
                    New Orleans - 366 hours 34 minutes

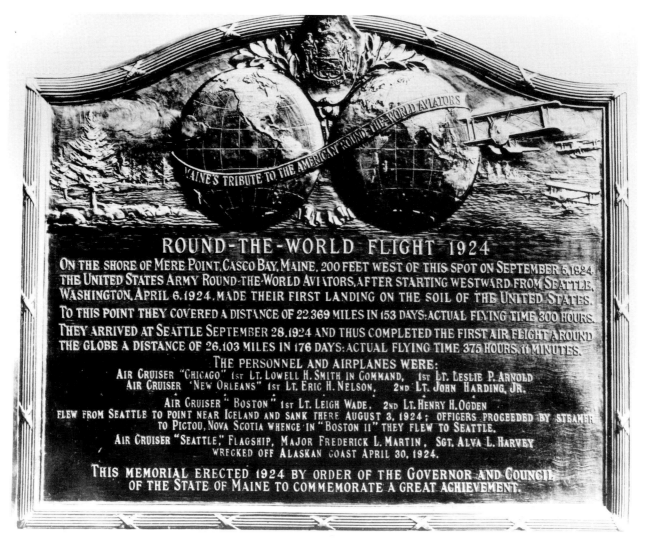

ROUND-THE-WORLD FLIGHT 1924

ON THE SHORE OF MERE POINT, CASCO BAY, MAINE, 200 FEET WEST OF THIS SPOT ON SEPTEMBER 5, 1924, THE UNITED STATES ARMY ROUND-THE-WORLD AVIATORS, AFTER STARTING WESTWARD FROM SEATTLE, WASHINGTON, APRIL 6, 1924, MADE THEIR FIRST LANDING ON THE SOIL OF THE UNITED STATES.

TO THIS POINT THEY COVERED A DISTANCE OF 22,369 MILES IN 153 DAYS: ACTUAL FLYING TIME 300 HOURS.

THEY ARRIVED AT SEATTLE SEPTEMBER 28, 1924 AND THUS COMPLETED THE FIRST AIR FLIGHT AROUND THE GLOBE A DISTANCE OF 26,103 MILES IN 176 DAYS: ACTUAL FLYING TIME 375 HOURS, 11 MINUTES.

THE PERSONNEL AND AIRPLANES WERE:
AIR CRUISER "CHICAGO" 1ST LT. LOWELL H. SMITH IN COMMAND, 1ST LT. LESLIE P. ARNOLD
AIR CRUISER "NEW ORLEANS" 1ST LT. ERIC H. NELSON, 2ND LT. JOHN HARDING, JR.

AIR CRUISER "BOSTON" 1ST LT. LEIGH WADE, 2ND LT. HENRY H. OGDEN
FLEW FROM SEATTLE TO POINT NEAR ICELAND AND SANK THERE AUGUST 3, 1924; OFFICERS PROCEEDED BY STEAMER TO PICTOU, NOVA SCOTIA WHENCE IN "BOSTON II" THEY FLEW TO SEATTLE.

AIR CRUISER "SEATTLE," FLAGSHIP, MAJOR FREDERICK L. MARTIN, SGT. ALVA L. HARVEY
WRECKED OFF ALASKAN COAST APRIL 30, 1924.

THIS MEMORIAL ERECTED 1924 BY ORDER OF THE GOVERNOR AND COUNCIL OF THE STATE OF MAINE TO COMMEMORATE A GREAT ACHIEVEMENT.

U.S. AIR FORCE MUSEUM

The world flight monument, located in front of the U.S. Coast Guard LORAN Station on Attu in the Aleutian Islands. There is one correction on the plaque: in 1924 it was the U.S. Army Air Service, not the U.S. Army Air Corps. PICTORIAL HISTORIES

This World Cruiser display is in the Museum of Flying, Seattle, Washington.

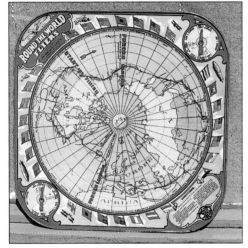

Although the world flight did not have the sustaining interest of the 1927 Lindbergh flight, this game, produced after the flight, shows that at least one company was trying to capitalize on the uniqueness of the adventure.

An older view of the New Orleans when it was at Dayton with the world fliers' sculpture.

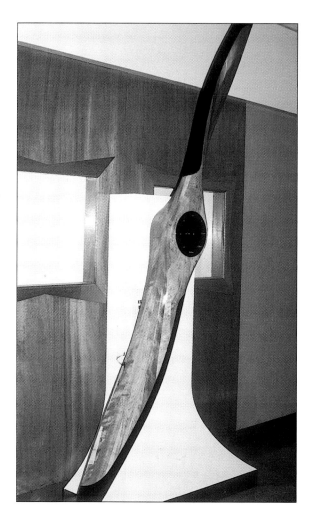

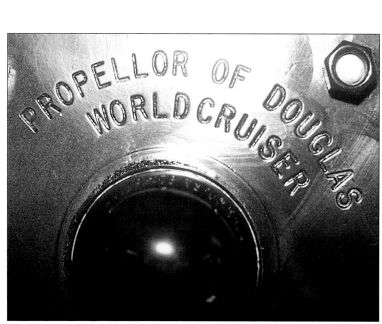

Erik Nelson's flight bag and the propeller of the Boston II *are on display at the History and Traditions Museum at Lackland AFB, San Antonio, Texas.*

The world flight monument at the entrance to the Naval Station Puget Sound (formerly the Sand Point Field and the Sand Point Naval Air Station).

Jake Allison of Burton, Ohio, owns Erik Nelson's flight jacket. Since Nelson was the pilot of the New Orleans *during the world flight, it can be assumed that he flew the* Boston II *sometime after the flight.*

The Liberty engine of the Seattle is now on display at the Alaska Aviation Heritage Museum in Anchorage. In the 1960s Bob Reeve, founder of Reeve Aleutian Airways, was instrumental in salvaging part of the wrecked airplane from its crash site. The engine was at the Alaska Transportation Museum in Palmer until 1993 when it was brought to Anchorage for permanent display. ALASKA AVIATION HERITAGE MUSEUM

Ted Spencer, director of the Alaska Aviation Heritage Museum, holds a tank from the Seattle. Other parts are also shown.

Lowell Thomas Jr. of Anchorage, Alaska, owns one of the control wheels from the Seattle.

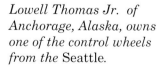

This beautiful diorama, made by Jamie and Larry Pye some years ago, depicts the Seattle *and the* Boston *tied up at a dock in Seward, Alaska.* U.S. AIR FORCE MUSEUM

Artifacts of Liet. Leigh Wade, on display at the Aviation Museum of Kentucky, Blue Grass Airport, Lexington, Kentucky.

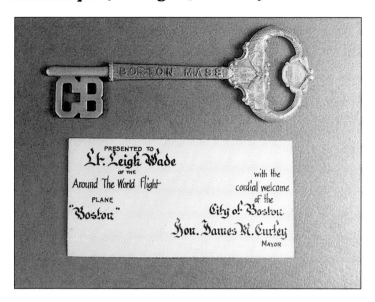

Cigarette case - *"Presented to Lieut. Leigh Wade, Air Service U.S. Army, by the citizens of Omaha Aviation Center of the United States. Pioneer Round the World Flight, September 27, 1924"*

"Dept of Mass. A.L. Boston, Sept. 1924"

"Presented to Lieut. Leigh Wade by the City of Muskogee for intrepid flying skill."

"Member, World Flight Hero, Lieut. Leigh Wade, Boy Scouts of L.A., 1924"

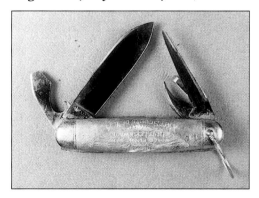

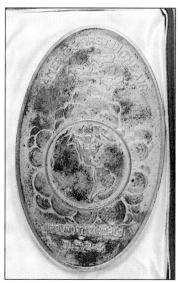

"America First in the Air, Around the World, 1924"

Two weeks before the world flight ended, a young museum aide named Paul E. Garber suggested that the Smithsonian Institution acquire one of the aircraft for its aviation collection. Eleven months later, the Secretary of War approved the transfer of the Chicago to the collection. On September 25, 1925, the Chicago made its final flight from McCook Field in Dayton, Ohio, to Bolling Field, Washington, D.C. The plane was soon placed on display at the Arts and Industries Building on the mall. When the new National Air and Space Museum opened on July 1, 1976, the Chicago, which had been restored, was placed in its present display area. NATIONAL AIR AND SPACE MUSEUM

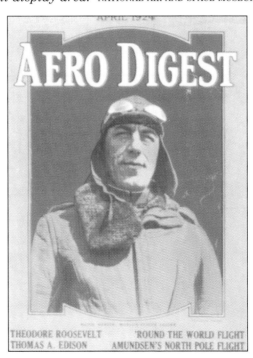

MUSEUM OF FLYING

Bibliography

Cunningham, Frank, *Skymaster. The Story of Donald Douglas.* Philadelphia: Dorrance & Co., 1943.

Glines, Carroll V. *Round–the-World Flights.* Princeton, N.J.: Van Nostrand Reinhold, 1982.

Gwynn-Jones, Terry. *Farther and Faster.* Washington, D.C.: Smithsonian Institution Press, 1991.

Maurer, Maurer. *Aviation in the U.S. Army, 1919–1939.* Washington, D.C.: Office of Air Force History, 1987.

McKay, Ernest A. *A World to Conquer. The Epic Story of the First Around-theWorld Flight.* New York: Aero, 1981.

Morrison, Wilbur H. *Donald W. Douglas: A Heart with Wings.* Ames: Iowa State University Press, 1991

Ruotsala, Jim. *Pilots of the Panhandle, Aviation In Southeast Alaska,* "The Early Years: 1920–1935. Juneau: Seadrome, 1997.

Thomas, Lowell. *The First World Flight.* Boston: Houghton Mifflin Co., 1925.

Wells, Linton. *Blood on the Moon: The Autobiography of Linton Wells.* Boston: Houghton Mifflin Co., 1937.

PETER M. BOWERS

About the Authors

Carroll V. Glines

Carroll V. Glines is a retired Air Force colonel who resides in Dallas, Texas. He began writing professionally on a free lance basis while in the service and is the author of 32 books and more than 750 articles for national magazines. After retirement from the Air Force in 1968, he was successively the associate editor of Armed Forces Management, and editor of Air Cargo, Air Line Pilot and Professional Pilot magazines. He has been listed in Who's Who in America since 1976 and has won writing awards from the Freedoms Foundation, Aviation/ Space Writers Association, Alaska Press Association, and International Association of Business Communicators. He was awarded the Max Steinbock Award for "Hu-

manistic spirit in journalism" in 1981 and the prestigious Lauren D. Lyman Award in 1984 for "Outstanding achievement in aviation writing." He has been Curator for the Doolittle Library at the University of Texas, Dallas since 1994.

Stan B. Cohen

Stan B. Cohen is a native of West Virginia and has a degree in geology from West Virginia University. After many years working as a geologist, ski shop operator and director of an historical park, he established Pictorial Histories Publish-

ing company in Missoula, Montana in 1976. Since then he has authored or coauthored 67 books and published over 250. Some of his aviation titles include: *The Alaska Flying Expedition; Flying Beats Work. A Pictorial History of Reeve Aleutian Airways; Hawaiian Airlines, a Pictorial History; Wings to the Orient;* and *Destination Tokyo, A Pictorial History of Doolittle's Tokyo Raid, April 18, 1942.* He lives in Missoula with his wife Anne and travels the world researching books and attending military reunions.

Cohen at the Attu monument,

Index
(Captions are not indexed.)